DUBAI

DUBAI

The Arabian Dream

BY DAVID SAUNDERS

TransGlobe Publishing

The Bedouin

I love the realm, this land, the Bedu in their hue
from all sides, left and right, is my destiny renewed

O Bedu, the true Arab, by your deeds and actions
your generosity and hospitality are your attractions

I love the land that breeds heroes from the sword
This dear land, its gracious day, its embracing nights

I love the Sheikh, this Leader of Men
Sheikh Zayed, his honest word, his promise kept

Known by all, from near and far
all Arabs speak of his generosity, his pride and his desires

I love hunting and riding, and the horse
the all night drinking of coffee, deep in discourse

I love the gazelle, eyes deep and black in Kohl
the sight healing the desert travellers so bold

Its long neck, its light hair comforting the weary, young and old
my soul soars like a bird, relaxing my being, alighting from the cold

In this dark desert of life that is lit by the stars
in a place where only deer wander the beyond

Over there are my hopes, the meaning and purpose of my life
renewal from the seasons, and from other's strife

Over there do I seek a truer life
and come back emptied of my troubles, and all my strife

Sheikh Mohammed bin Rashid Al Maktoum
The Crown Prince of Dubai

لوحة بدوية

أحب أهلي والبدو والشوق قتّال
منهم يميني للزّمان وشمالي

البدو يا أصل العرب قول وأفعال
أهل المروة والكرم والتّزالي

وأحب أرضٍ تنبت اسيوف وابطال
أرضٍ عزيزة عن صروف الليالي

وأحب شيخٍ صادق بفعل واقوال
الشّيخ زايد هو زعيم الرجالي

زايد سجلّه بالمفاخر و لفضال
عند العرب معروف أوّل وتالي

واهوى القنص والهجن واكون خيّال
وأسهر على فنجان بنٍّ وهالي

وأحب ظبيٍ اكحل العين يفتال
يشفيك شوفه من اريام الرمالي

واشقر طويل المعنّق يشرح البال
له كل ماحان الهدد طاب فالي

في صحصح قفرٍ بها يلمع اللّال
وفي خايعٍ ما فيه غير الغزالي

هناك تتجدد معاني وآمال
وارد خالي من همومي وسال

الشّيخ محمد بن راشد آل مكتوم

TransGlobe Publishing Limited
72 New Bond Street
London W1S 1RR

First published by
TransGlobe Publishing Ltd. 2003
© 2003 TransGlobe Publishing Ltd.

Text and captions copyright
© 2003 David Saunders
© Photographic copyright see page 207

ISBN 0 9545083 0 0

A CIP catalogue for this book is available
from the British Library

Designed by Struktur Design
Reprographics by The Saxon Group, England
Printed in Singapore by CS Graphics

CONTENTS

LEFT:
Inspired by the sails of lateen-rigged Arab dhows, the design of the Creek Golf and Yacht Club is reminiscent of the Sydney Opera House.

BELOW
In the mid-nineteenth century 335 pearling boats of varying sizes operated out of Dubai. This deep-sea sambuk is on display at Dubai Museum.

Falconry was adopted in the Arabian Peninsula as a means of supplementing the local diet with birds and small prey of the desert. Today, falconry is still a popular sport, with members of the Ruling Family amongst its staunchest practitioners.

The ornate Jumeirah Mosque is one of the most beautiful in the region. Built of stone with two minarets and a large central dome, it conforms to the medieval Fatimid style of design.

*The taller of the two
Emirates Towers on
Sheikh Zayed Road
reaches 350 metres
(1,148 feet) – the
tallest building
in Europe and
Middle East.*

FOLLOWING PAGE
*The jagged ridges of
the Hajar Mountains
extend into the
United Arab
Emirates from Oman,
where they rise
to 2,000 metres
(6,560 feet).*

INTRODUCTION

"The living man, or more exactly, a man who deserves to live, is the one who works for the present and the future of his country and adds new glories to those made by his fathers and grandfathers."
(Sheikh Rashid bin Saeed Al Maktoum, Ruler of Dubai 1958-1990).

Dubai's rags-to-riches story has moved on a chapter or two since those early days when Sheikh Rashid bin Saeed Al Maktoum, the late Ruler and recognised father of modern Dubai, laid the foundations for the Sheikhdom's road to prosperity. Far from being an end in itself, Dubai's wealth has provided the means to pursue the more far-reaching dream of its Rulers and its people.

On the face of it there seems little reason why Dubai should be so wildly successful in an area of the world where disquiet and instability are the norm. Its inhospitable desert is separated from a shallow sea by marshland and salt flats. Blisteringly hot in summer, the land offers no drinkable surface water and no shade from the elements other than a few palm trees in widely scattered oases.

How, then, did this unpromising desert outpost become transformed into one of the world's most dynamic and cosmopolitan centres of trade, commerce and tourism? The answer does not lie in the oil, of which Dubai's share has been comparatively small in relation to its neighbours in the region. One must dig deeper in the sands of time for the answers.

For most of human existence, much of this desiccated terrain bordering the notoriously hostile Empty Quarter has proved an almost impenetrable barrier between Africa and Asia. Ever since civilisation in Mesopotamia's Fertile Crescent (present day Iraq) first began looking to foreign lands for trade and commerce some 7,000 years ago, this coastline of the Arabian Peninsula has attracted passing interest from merchants travelling to the Indus Valley. And it was not long before the few early settlers found ways of harnessing these trickles of trade and turning them into profit.

Nature, whilst harsh in the extreme, has still provided this region of the Gulf with a few attributes that have enabled its more resourceful inhabitants to survive and prosper. As technology and social conditions have evolved, Dubai's entrepreneurs have been able to convert nature's good fortune into benefit.

Boat building, sailing and navigational skills; pearling, gold and trading skills and the more recent advent of plentiful energy resources have enabled the locals to reach beyond their natural horizons, further than anything their size and numbers would normally permit. But that is the nature of Dubai, with no ambition beyond reach, and no lack of energy to pursue the dream of Ruler and ruled alike to become the jewel of the Arabian Gulf.

Successive guardians of the land have pursued the people's desire for security, autonomy and wealth within the scope of available opportunities. The pursuit of the Arabian dream has enabled Dubai to grow from humble beginnings, enduring times of incredible hardship, to become the burgeoning Emirate which can today track its progress on an exponential curve.

The challenges of the past are embodied in the dangers of external threats, the harshness of nature and paucity of resources, which turned life into a daily struggle for survival. Why has Dubai managed to transform itself to this modern and bustling centre of culture, business, commerce, banking and tourism? And how will it meet the challenges of the future in a troubled and fast-changing region?

Dubai stands on the edge of the vast and inhospitable Empty Quarter (Rub'Al Khali) that stretches some 300,000 square kilometres over the Arabian Peninsula. Wind-blown sand dunes advance across the desert at an average rate of 60 centimetres a year.

THE LAND

"It is a bitter, desiccated land which knows nothing of gentleness and ease, yet men have lived here since earliest times."
(*Arabian Sands* by Wilfred Thesiger, London, 1959)

Dubai occupies a small wedge of the eastern corner of the Arabian Peninsula – nearly 3,900 square kilometres (1,506 square miles) – straddling the Tropic of Cancer. The town embraces the largest natural creek along the coastline. Without this nine-mile tongue of the Gulf reaching into the desert, there would be no reason for Dubai to have come into existence. The Creek (*al Khor*) has played a pivotal role in providing a magnet for early trade and commerce.

The Gulf is some 1,000 kilometres (620 miles) long and nearly 340 kilometres (210 miles) wide, reaching a maximum depth of 110 metres (360 feet). It experiences few storms and is more easily navigable than the neighbouring Red Sea.

Dubai is the second largest of the seven Emirates comprising the United Arab Emirates (UAE) that together cover a total of 78,000 square kilometres (30,000 square miles). Two-thirds of this land is desert, and includes rolling dunes and salt flats (*sabkha* – impacted salt and sand). The remainder comprises mountains, river valleys and urban areas. It is an environment that marks the edge of an overflow of sand from the Empty Quarter to the south. The Empty Quarter or *Rub' Al Khali*, is the world's largest sand desert, spread over 300,000 square kilometres.

Summer (May – September) is hot and humid. Daytime temperatures rarely fall below 40 degree Centigrade (104 degrees Fahrenheit), and the sand can reach 80 degrees Centigrade. The sun attacks from overhead and its heat reflects off the sand and rock. Humidity, especially near the coast, generally exceeds 60 per cent and can frequently touch 90 per cent.

In winter, daytime temperatures hover around 30 degrees Centigrade (mid-80s Fahrenheit) and humidity falls to more bearable levels. At night, desert temperatures plummet to bone-chilling levels.

To the east of Dubai the igneous and limestone peaks of the Hajar Mountains that rise to about 2,000 metres (6,560 feet) present a natural barrier between the east and west coasts of the UAE. This topographical barricade traps most of the rain-water that tries to cross over from the deep, relatively cool waters of the Indian Ocean. Rainfall over the mountains replenishes the underground water-table on which the population has relied for most of its history.

Much of the meagre annual average rainfall of 42mm (1.65in) to the west of the mountains is sudden and torrential, falling in sporadic deluges between January and March when the landscape is totally transformed.

A heavy grey canopy is drawn across the sky and the air smells strangely different before a cloudburst. Often years pass with only negligible drizzles of precipitation, but occasionally, the muted drumming of approaching rain crescendos and the desert, ever constant and unyielding, is changed from the hostility of heat to the oppression of a brief cloudburst. *Wadis* – dry river valleys – turn into cascading rivers. The sand soaks up these floods like a sponge as dormant seeds and hardy sedges awaken to new life.

In the foothills of the Hajar Mountains lies a small enclave of land surrounded by territory belonging to Oman, Ras Al Khaimah and Ajman. Although physically detached from the rest of the Emirate, the community of Hatta is administered by Dubai.

Just across the border in Oman, Hatta Pools are sunken within a parched and eerie prehistoric landscape. The spring pools, along an otherwise dry river-bed, provide one of the few examples of natural surface water on the Arabian Peninsula.

Harsh as it is, the landscape is not barren. The mountains support a rich sprinkling of flora, including oleander and euphorbia, acacia and fig trees, while the skies are patrolled by eagles, kestrels, ravens, swifts and crag martins.

Of the 400 species of bird found here, some 90 are resident breeds. In October and March, Dubai witnesses the north-south migrations between Europe and Africa, and east-west migrations between India and the Near East. In winter, flamingos from the lakes of northern Iran make their home on the upper reaches of the Creek, where tidal wetlands provide a stopover for herons, ducks and shore birds that feed on the mudflats.

The *houbara* bustard, preferred prey of falconers, has been hunted almost to extinction. Similarly, populations of Arabian wolf, caracal, jackal, hyena, oryx, gazelle and *tahr* (mountain goat) fared well in this desert before being decimated by hunters during the last century.

Today, some of the proceeds of oil and trade have been diverted into conservation projects that are successfully restoring depleted species.

In the foothills of the Hajar Mountains are scattered many wadis *where springs emerge from the desiccated landscape. Meagre rainfall is sufficient to sustain hardy vegetation such as scrub brush, euphorbia, acacia, a few fig trees and* wadi *grasses.*

Sparse vegetation clings to shifting sands. In some places the water-table nears the surface, within reach of the plant's roots. In others, the leaves catch enough of the overnight dew to survive. These desert sedges are the main source of nutrition for wandering camels.

Further down the food chain, desert fauna includes gerbils, foxes, hares, skinks, scorpions, spiders, beetles, snakes and lizards. Herbivores can choose from a menu of more than 600 species of wild plants, though urban development and recreation activities are taking their toll on this astonishingly rich diversity.

In the warm, saline waters of the Gulf, sea grasses provide food for marine species such as the elusive dugong – the only known marine mammalian herbivore. Several species of turtle, notably the green turtle and hawksbill, nest on the beaches of islands in the Gulf. Some 50 days after the eggs are laid in the sand, baby turtles emerge and scuttle towards the sea, with only a fraction surviving the gauntlet of winged and finned predators.

Just as flora and fauna have learnt to adapt and evolve over the millennia, so has man found ways to thrive in some of earth's harshest settings.

THE BIRTH OF A PEOPLE

"These tribesmen are accustomed since birth to the physical hardships of the desert, to drink the scanty bitter water of the Sands, to eat gritty unleavened bread, to endure the maddening irritation of driven sand, intense cold, heat, and blinding glare in a land without shade or cloud."
(Wilfred Thesiger)

Within the history of this austere land lies a mythology that underwrites the lives of all the people of Dubai today. This mythology encompasses a resilient, pioneering spirit that embraces the unremitting harshness of the desert and the unknown hazards of adventure across the seas

In much the same way as the spirit of the Samurai lives on in Japanese culture and the undercurrents of the Outback run through the veins of many an Australian, so too does the legacy of the desert still burn in the hearts of even the most sophisticated urban Arab in Dubai.

This inherited memory takes as its source a pride in courage, strength and endurance. It engenders a collective dream that was born at a time when the cruel finality of the desert allowed only the fittest to survive. Each man was condemned to live within the confines of his ingenuity. There is an Arab saying which defines this spirit: "Polish comes from the town, wisdom from the desert".

Twenty-first century Dubai city dwellers take pride in their desert past.

Before the onset of cities, the land provided few redeeming features to offer respite from this arduous existence. Other than sun, sand and sea the north-east wing of the Arabian Peninsula had never been blessed with great natural resources. Yet, for such an apparently barren strip of land, a surprising number of people have wanted to control it – Persians, Ottomans, Portuguese, French, Germans and British.

Other than the fish and pearls harvested from the sea, the land itself offered only a very frugal existence, reliant mainly on converting the fruit of the date palm and meagre livestock into food, clothing and shelter.

Some inhabitants, though, managed to raise their own lives above subsistence levels by looking beyond their own shores. Through the ages, these people have watched the loose threads of foreign civilisations pass through their land, treating the area as an inconvenient stopover en route to more hospitable climes.

LEFT
Archaeological excavations at Al Qusais to the north-east of the city of Dubai unearthed earthen pots, bronze arrowheads, hooks and needles dating back 4,000 years.

RIGHT
Sailing vessels have plied the waters of the Gulf for millennia, providing a means for trade and exploration, and giving this region one of the richest and most colourful seafaring traditions in the world. This qutiyah was returning to Dubai from East Africa in the 1950s.

In the fourth century BC, troops from Alexander the Great's army returned this way from the battlefields of the Indian subcontinent. Traders have pitched camp here for millennia and left their mark. In the late sixteenth century the Portuguese, out to plunder India's riches, tried to usurp control of the lucrative Gulf trading routes from the Persians. Their French and Dutch successors followed suit in the seventeenth and eighteenth centuries, while the British tempered their passion for power and plunder with a modicum of commitment to the local Rulers.

The first airline passengers in the 1930s used the Creek in Dubai as a staging post between London and Australia. Today Dubai International Airport has become one of the world's busiest and most advanced aerial hubs, the regional centre for air traffic between East and West.

By contrast, the appearance of Islam in the seventh century was neither transient nor superficial. Following his first Revelation in 610AD, the Prophet Muhammad called for the worship of one God – "There is no other god but God" – and his teaching was based on charity, equality and neighbourly love. Islam has imprinted its mark on the souls and lives of succeeding generations of Arabs in the region.

Successive waves of exotic influences touched the shores, enriching the land. Besides providing goods and materials to make life more comfortable, trade exposed Dubai to different cultures, enabling small, isolated and often nomadic communities to develop into today's sophisticated, worldly citizens with a modern global outlook.

The story begins some 1,000 kilometres (620 miles) to the north-west in the Fertile Crescent of Mesopotamia, between the Tigris and Euphrates Rivers. As the inhabitants of this rich delta advanced from food foraging to agriculture and animal husbandry, they were freed from the tyranny of a hand-to-mouth existence and in time began to look beyond their own shores for life-enriching goods to trade.

Archaeological finds along the coast of what is now the UAE reveal distinctive Neolithic black pottery from 'Ubaid in Mesopotamia dating back 7,000 years. The Gulf has been an effective corridor for trade, giving this region probably the richest and longest-operating seafaring traditions in the world.

Sumerians from southern Mesopotamia scoured the shores of the Gulf in search of copper to trade for manufactured goods. Sumerian texts

describe an ancient, wealthy land called Magan that corresponds approximately with present day Oman and the UAE. During the Bronze Age, the Magan civilisation yielded copper, minerals and semi-precious stones. Excavations at Al Qusais on the north-east outskirts of Dubai unearthed 4,000 year-old bronze arrow heads, hooks and needles.

The chronicled voyages of Sinbad the Sailor highlight the restless spirit of adventure and the pioneering drive that took pagan Arabs across distant seas and endless deserts. The legendary Arab navigator Ahmed Ibn Majid – the 'Lion of the Sea' – was born in the 1430s near Ras Al Khaimah to the north of Dubai, and travelled extensively between the Gulf, India and East Africa. Arab sailors developed the astrolabe – an instrument to aid navigation on oceans away from the sight of land. The West has learnt rudimentary navigational skills from the Arabs, in addition to algebra, astronomy and basic medical skills.

Sinbad – a merchant rather than sailor – invested extravagantly in goods to trade on his voyages. His travels took him to far-flung islands in the Gulf and into the Arabian Sea in search of fabulous adventures that invariably involved gold and treasure, and a shipwreck or two.

"I was suddenly seized with a longing to travel the world again, and to make myself another fortune by trading. And so I took a great purse of gold and bought myself a wealth of merchandise and everything I needed for my voyage … The journey gave me plentiful opportunities for further trade. In the lands of Hind and Sind I bought cloves and ginger and all kinds of exotic spices. These Indian seas afforded us countless wonders." (*The Seven Voyages of Sinbad the Sailor*, retold by John Yeoman, Pavilion Books, 1998)

In 1977, the Norwegian anthropologist Thor Heyerdahl chose a practical demonstration to prove that this level of trade was possible with the technology of ancient times. Referring to the oldest Sumerian illustrations of their sailing craft, he constructed a replica from reeds found in the Tigris-Euphrates delta. Together with eleven companions, Heyerdahl sailed his vessel – *Tigris* – from Mesopotamia to Bahrain, then Oman and on to the Indus Valley in Pakistan, then back to Aden.

The sailors of Magan commanded a strategic position at the mouth of the Gulf, beginning to dominate trade between Mesopotamia and India from some 3,000 years ago.

Around this time traders from the Minaean civilisation in north-east Yemen brought frankincense from Dhaufar to market in Egypt and Syria.

The Greek writer Herodotus travelled throughout much of the Achaemenid (Persian) Empire, and described Arabia in his *Histories*. "Arabia is the last of inhabited lands towards the south, and it is the only country which produces frankincense, myrrh, cassia, cinnamon, and laudanum."

For centuries the Egyptians, Assyrians and Seleucids fought to control the desert route along which frankincense was carried north from the incense groves of Yemen and southern Oman. Early writers (including the Romans), impressed by the wealth born of trade, referred to the region as *Arabia Felix* – Arabia the Fortunate, or *Arabia Odifera* – Perfumed Arabia.

In 24BC Emperor Augustus sent an army commanded by Aelius Gallus, prefect for Egypt, to conquer the lands where the valuable *Gum Arabica* originated. The quest failed and troops retreated after marching through the desert for 1,450 kilometres (900 miles). This was the sole attempt made by a European power to invade Arabia in classical times.

Meanwhile, ancient clay tablets tell of ships carrying herbs and spices, frankincense and myrrh, textiles, ceramics, gems and jewellery. Teak, cedar and sandalwood came from India, along with ebony, spices, silk and precious stones. From Africa came ivory, horn, cinnamon, aromatics and slaves. In return, cloth and clothing, aromatics, incense, glass, metalwork, weapons, tools, wine and grain were shipped to the Near East and India.

Baked clay tablets found in archaeological sites in present day Iraq reveal commercial records of merchants trading throughout the region well before the invention of money. Letters of credit enabled merchants far from home to barter for goods. Funds were provided to the captains of vessels trading on their own account, with the share of profits agreed beforehand.

There was, though, one highly tradable item that outlasted even frankincense. This jewel of history originated within the Gulf itself – a little stone that appeared naturally in a variety of shapes, sizes and colours. It set the pulse of the Queen of Sheba racing; Cleopatra adorned herself with it and Queen Victoria treasured her pearls. Queen Zenobia (Ruler of Palmyra, situated in present day Syria) apparently declared war against the Roman Empire in order to monopolise this irregular gem.

The tiny treasure provided a livelihood for a large proportion of the population, bringing wealth that in turn generated more trade and expansion. For nearly 3,000 years the world's finest pearls and mother-of-pearl formed

Returning to home port after the rigours of a four-month pearling season at sea was a joyous occasion for the pearl fishermen.

the backbone of the region's economy, and the only export commodity.

Oysters flourished in the warm shallow waters of the Gulf down to a depth of about 35 metres. Pearl oysters are salt-water molluscs (*Meleagrina*), a completely different species to the edible oyster. Up to 100 young oysters may cling to a single leaf of sea grass, from which they extract nutrients. When larger, they fix onto a rock on the seabed, feeding on plankton through their gill-filaments.

A pearl is born as a result of an irritation, such as a grain of sand that enters the filament of the oyster shell. A nacreous layer, produced naturally by the mollusc, wraps itself around the intruder, thus forming a tiny pearl that grows as the secretions build layer upon layer.

Arab legend asserts that a pearl is formed when the mollusc rises to the surface of the sea during a hailstorm, opens its shell to catch a hailstone or drop of rain, then returns to the bottom of the ocean where the secretions around it form a beautiful pearl.

The finest pearls are smooth and round with a brilliant skin, pinkish-rose colour and faint undertone of cream. Pearls come in many colours – grey, bronze, black, yellow, lavender, orange, brown, blue and green – but cream and white are most popular. A hole is drilled through the centre of the pearl by hand, a skilled task only performed by experienced craftsmen.

Harvesting pearls was a highly organised operation, fraught with danger and discomfort. A seasonal activity, pearling took place between the months of May and September each year when the seas are warm and calm.

While the dhows were caulked – made watertight – by treating the boat timbers with fish oil or tar, teams of divers (often slaves) assembled from many quarters. Those who spent the rest of the year fishing, tending date palms, goats or camels, building boats or labouring gravitated to the coast to seek work on the pearling boats. Anyone who could climb palm trees was adept at climbing a boat's rigging.

The day on the pearling banks began for the divers with a handful of dates and a sip of water or black coffee. Wearing nothing but a bone or wooden nose-clip or nose-plug (*fatam*) and carrying a stone weight attached to their ankles to enable them to descend, they plunged down repeatedly to fill their baskets (*diyyan*) with oyster shells. Between dives, they rested holding onto ropes from the boat. Every hour they climbed back into the boat to rest. In one day, each diver might dive 60 times for up to 90 seconds at a time.

In search of the priceless pearl, divers endured a physically punishing regime. With a nose-clip, basket and a stone weight to aid their descent, divers made up to 60 dives a day.

The fruit of centuries of labour. Pearls in the Sultan Al Owais Collection displayed at the National Bank of Dubai's dedicated Pearl Museum. The late Sultan Al Owais, one of Dubai's legendary businessmen and pearl merchants, and a founding partner of the National Bank of Dubai, left this unique collection for permanent display at the Bank's HQ building on Dubai Creek.

The main meal of the day came after sunset, as the oysters were opened early next morning under the supervision of the captain (*nukhada*) who registered the haul.

On average boats carried eight divers, 10 haulers and an apprentice to catch the fish, cook and clean. The largest boats might also have had a *mutawwa* (a religious teacher) who led prayers and rhythmic chants and choruses to raise morale. The songs were of the sea and infused with the lilting rhythm of the waves.

Conditions on the boats were cramped and offered no luxuries. A diet of fresh fish and rice was washed down with sparse quantities of sweet water and coffee.

In the sea, sharks, barracuda and sea snakes were the least of the divers' worries. More prolific were the large jellyfish that inflict a painful sting, producing a fever lasting several days. Divers were given some protection by wearing a one-piece cotton suit when jellyfish were around.

All wounds were cauterised using a red-hot iron, while the patient breathed in frankincense smoke. During the treatment, a verse from the Koran was recited to drive out the *jinns* – evil spirits – from those afflicted by the stresses of diving.

The pearling boats often stayed at sea for the entire season of about 120 days, replenishing fresh water supplies at Dalma Island. Pearl dealers, *tawash*, who bought and sold pearls, often approached the boats at sea or when they moored on the island.

Initially, pearls found a ready market in India and the Far East. They later became fashionable in Britain and throughout the rest of Europe and across the Atlantic. New York was second only to Bombay as a market for Gulf pearls in the two opening decades of the twentieth century.

From the beginning of the Islamic era, Dubai was an established trading transit point for dhows between India, East Africa and the Northern Gulf, and camel caravans between Iraq and Oman. People drawn to the caravans built permanent settlements along the routes. Jumeirah, some 15 kilometres south-west of the city of Dubai, was a caravan station linking the ancient city of Ctesiphon, now situated in present day Iraq, with northern Oman. Today, Jumeirah forms the hub of the Emirate's booming tourist industry, with 'caravans' of Europeans decamping in luxury hotels, the likes of which no ancient could have ever dreamed.

In the sixteenth century, pearling began to attract the greed of colonialists. In 1588, the Italian explorer Gasparo Balbi described Dubai as a prosperous place largely dependent on pearling. The Portuguese conquered the kingdom of Hormuz, which administered the Gulf coast, ruthlessly dominating the region for a century to use as their stepping-stone to India.

The Portuguese themselves were in turn expelled from Hormuz in 1622 by Shah Abbas of Persia, with support from the British East India Company. Britain finally drove out all their colonial competitors, becoming the principal colonial maritime power in the Gulf from the mid-nineteenth century onwards. This marked the beginning of an extended, ambivalent relationship between Britain and the inhabitants of the coastlands. They provided some order and infrastructure to the region, while pursuing their own trading interests bound up with an imperial agenda.

Much of the local population comprised nomadic tribes of desert Arabs living by a strict code of honour (*miruwa or muru'a*). This code embodied manly excellence, courage, chivalry and gallantry. Each man was bound to be hospitable, generous, proud, shrewd, loyal and patient in the face of adversity. An Arab Bedouin would always be willing to offer food and shelter to a travelling stranger, while ready to sacrifice his life to preserve his personal and family honour, or that of the tribe.

Each tribe was divided into clans made up of several family groups. The bond of clanship – *asabiyya* – was centred on blood relatives, yet welcomed and absorbed freed slaves and outsiders seeking refuge. Each member believed in the munificence of the universe, with a strong sense of being a part of the whole.

The Arab Bedu is both a consensual democrat and a spiritual aristocrat. He meets nobility on an equal footing, while also viewing the Arabian nation as the noblest of all. He takes pride in the purity of his bloodline, his eloquence, his poetry, his sword, his horse and above all, his noble ancestry. The Arab prizes his lineage more highly than many other races.

The coming of Islam reinforced, rather than disrupted this tribal system, helping social cohesion and strengthening the common will in the face of adversity. Frauke Heard-Bey writes in her comprehensive book, *From Trucial States to United Arab Emirates*: "The common knowledge, understanding and acceptance of God's laws has been one of the fundamental reasons for the cohesion of the society in this area ... Islam has taken the sting out of the pre-Islamic tribal system of compulsory revenge for any

A hunting party of the late Sheikh Rashid bin Saeed Al Maktoum, Ruler of Dubai 1958-1990, at Nahl Duee on the outskirts of Dubai (c. 1950). On Sheikh Rashid's lap is Sheikha Ra'issa bint Khalifa Al Maktoum.

and every injury, by introducing forgiveness as a praiseworthy act. It has levelled the difference between members of different tribes by making them brothers in the same creed; it has changed the status of women, who in pre-Islamic times were often considered merely as objects of possession. Above all, Islam has brought to the tribal society a law which has its point of reference outside the tribal structure."

Having learnt to cope with one of the most punishing environments on earth, the Bedouin of the Arabian Peninsula developed a resilience and fortitude that makes light of hardship and takes upheaval in its stride. *Mafi moshkelah* – No problem – is the most common refrain in answer to any question or problem.

Today, the new prosperity is handled with equal stoicism. Conspicuous spending is certainly evident amongst most of the people, but not the irresponsible extravagance that fails to value the past and neglects the need to nourish the future.

It is this steely, steadfast resolve that has informed their most important decisions and enabled them to overcome fear of change. Life-threatening challenges come with the terrain. Each situation is judged, measured and negotiated.

The nomadic lifestyle does not welcome excess baggage. Possessions were kept to a minimum – saddles, ropes, water-skins, cooking pots, daggers (*khanjars*), ragged clothes and rifles comprised the bulk of the Bedu family's worldly goods.

Thesiger wrote in *The Arabian Sands*: "They lived in black tents in the desert, or in bare rooms devoid of furnishings in the villages and towns. They had no taste, nor inclination for refinements. Most of them demanded only the bare necessities of life, enough food and drink to keep them alive, clothes to cover their nakedness, some form of shelter from the sun and wind, weapons, a few pots, rugs, water-skins, and their saddlery. It was a life which produced much that was noble, nothing that was gracious."

In summer, when the heat haze shimmered in the 50s Centigrade and life proceeded in slow motion, people lived in *Al Arish* (palm leaf) shelters built on low sand hills. They drank warm, slightly salty milk drawn from the udders of camels and goats. Water was drawn from wells that penetrated the water-table, which, if drained too quickly, turned brackish and had to be left to 'recover'.

During winter, the Bedu migrated into the desert erecting broad, low tents made from animal hair and skins. At night, they slept shrouded in the cloaks they wore while their horses and camels were hobbled to deter them from wandering too far from the camp.

Cloth was stretched between poles to catch what little rain might fall and channel it through a hole into a goat-skin container. Tribesmen also slung rags over thorn bushes at night, then squeezed out the dew absorbed during the colder dark hours. Even the gastric juices from the stomach of the hunted oryx was drunk in extreme circumstances.

Cultivated areas were irrigated by *aflaj* (singular *falaj*), a method of tapping springs and directing the water across plains that dates back thousands of years. The more elaborate systems carried water by gravity over long distances through channels both above and below ground. In places, bullocks drew the *mihale* to raise well water to feed the irrigation channels. Some of the old irrigation systems were brought into use again in the mid-twentieth century to reinvigorate agriculture and to extend the range and scope of cultivation.

Throughout recorded time, the date palm (*Phoenix dactylifera*) has been the 'prince of trees', supplying the population with high-calorie food and shelter from its bark and fronds. Tolerant of salty conditions, this noble tree thrives in intense heat. In many areas young trees need watering by hand until the roots tap into the water-table. Sprouting lower branches are trimmed annually, forming a trunk. After three or four years the tree flowers and the female tree is hand-pollinated with the panicles from a male tree. The harvesting of dates takes place between June and October.

Palm tree trunks were used as supporting beams in the houses while the stripped and bound branches became walls and the fibrous bark made strong rope and good padding. Citrus trees were often grown among the date palms, and latterly mangoes, figs and bananas.

Fish provided one of the only protein sources for most of the population. Fishermen constructed small boats (*shashah*) from the branches of date palms. Larger wooden boats (*amlah*) had sails and oars and could hold a crew of 25 men.

For many centuries, horses, camels and goats provided the triad of desert survival aids and these animals' lives were invariably intertwined with the welfare of the Bedouin themselves.

Until the advent of a regular police force, Sheikhs each retained their own personal guards to protect against raiding parties. Here, the late Sheikh Rashid stands at Jebel Ali with some of his retainers and Ronald Codrai at a cairn marking the spot for the second wildcat well to be drilled on the Trucial Coast.

Besides supplying milk and meat, goats provided material for essentials such as goat-skin buckets and tents, and coarse, black, goat-hair knitted socks that protected the feet from the hot sand.

Camels, one-humped dromedaries domesticated over 3,000 years ago, converted the desert sedge (*Calligonum*) into milk. Their skins were used to make tents, their dried dung burnt as fuel and, as beasts of burden, they provided the engine of land-based trade. It was not without good reason that these graceful beasts were called *Ata Allah* – a Gift from God.

Female camels were ridden for choice, while bulls made pack animals. Many male camels were killed at birth so that food was not wasted on them. In more recent times, *alfalfa* has been cultivated to provide consistently nutritious camel food.

But the haughty dromedary can be a moody and supercilious companion, roaring and snarling as packs are loaded onto its back. A kick from a camel can shatter bones or worse, a bite inflicts a serious wound and the smell of half-chewed cud spat out as a sign of displeasure is not pleasant in the least.

When couched, the camel's forelegs may be tied with the end of the head-rope to prevent it from rising. While standing, a restraining cord is attached to a nose-peg. And during raids where stealth was paramount, their mouths were tied to keep them quiet.

A camel can drink up to 12 gallons of water at a time, yet it can exist in winter for up to six months with no water as long as there is access to the most sparse desert grazing.

The Bedu also owe a great debt to their horse. For over 2,000 years, the Arabian horse's loyalty and toughness has contributed to the well-being of people in this part of the world. Looked after by the Bedu with as much kindness and attention as was given their wives and children, the horse was fed on dates and camel milk. In fact, the fresh morning milk was first fed to the horse before others of the family quenched their thirst. The horse grew to trust its handler and establish a close bond with its owner, faithful unto death. Many are the desert's romantic but true stories around wounded riders escaping battle on their steeds who rode themselves to death to save their master.

Bred for endurance and stamina rather than pure speed, the Arabian horse had to be able to take the rider into battle in raids of up to 120 kilometres (75 miles), and still have the strength to return home afterwards.

Bedouin of Arabia rode two men to a camel leading riderless horses into raids or battle, only mounting their steeds for the final charge while the horses were still fresh. The Bedu often rode without saddles or stirrups, with only a halter held in the left hand.

Horse racing in the region began in pre-Islamic times. The Bedouin tribes valued their horses above all other possessions, and demonstrated their skill and daring especially at celebrations such as *Eid El-Fitr* to mark the end of Ramadan.

Today, Dubai has 15 racing stables and horses are kept mainly for sport and competition. Flat racing covers distances of between 1 and 2.4 kilometres, whilst endurance races, the most challenging and gruelling of all equine activities for both rider and mount, involve long distances with upwards of 100 horses and as many four-wheel-drive vehicles in pursuit.

There are four stages of the local 205-kilometre endurance rides, which are closely supervised by medical teams and riders are shadowed by support vehicles. Covering up to 100 kilometres (62 miles) in eight hours, the Dubai courses pass through deep sand and surfaces as compact and hard as concrete.

On the international stage, Dubai is increasingly showing its winning colours. Sheikh Mohammed bin Rashid Al Maktoum, Dubai's Crown Prince, is himself a world champion endurance rider. He and his sons can be seen in almost every major race competing for honours against the world's best riders, and against each other. One of the sons, Sheikh Ahmed, won the 160-kilometre World Endurance Championship in 2002 on the Australian horse Bowman, against riders from 35 countries.

Arab horse breeders traditionally kept mares almost exclusively. Stallions were usually slaughtered at birth or sold when young. The Arabian horse can be moody, temperamental and difficult to train, yet selective crossbreeding between the five main strains of *asil* (pure-bred) horses have produced over 200 named bloodlines over the past two thousand years.

Raiding parties were frequent in lawless times when the desert Arab was called upon to defend the honour of his tribe, or to seek food, or to plunder. Inter-tribal battles, *Ayyam Al-'Arab*, were lethal games of tit for tat, often escalating into long-running eye-for-an-eye vendettas lasting decades or even centuries. Bands of Bedouin repeatedly launched raids against each other to increase their own wealth and power, and avenge the predatory raids of their enemies. Camels and horses were usually the most coveted booty. Women and children were unharmed, although they were sometimes carried off as part of the prize.

Camel raids became more deadly in the 1850s with the introduction of breech-loading rifles. Medical treatment was restricted to herbs, potions concocted from camels' urine and the use of a red-hot iron. All maladies, from headaches to intestinal troubles, were treated by branding or cauterising the stomach, chest or back of the patient. Older Bedu still bear scars from this time-honoured remedy, unchanged for thousands of years until the advent of modern medicine. While this painful remedy was being administered, soothing verses were recited from the Koran.

Rich pickings of trade on both land and sea proved irresistible to marauding tribes and ruthless pirates, and their activities earned this stretch of the Gulf the title of the Pirate Coast. By the beginning of the nineteenth century, the Qawasim of Ras Al Khaimah and Sharjah had a large, troublesome fleet of sailing vessels. Greed motivated a succession of attacks mainly by the Qawasim tribe, disrupting the rhythm of trading life in the region. The British, whose own ships had been plundered by the marauders, finally put a stop to the whole practice by destroying the entire Qasimi fleet in 1819.

As late as the 1940s it was still considered safer to travel by sea as Bedu raiding parties made travel overland hazardous. When Wilfred Thesiger crossed the Empty Quarter (*Rub' Al Khali*) in 1948 from the Yemen to Abu Dhabi, he noted the fortifications constructed as defences against such marauding tribes. "As we came out of the red dunes on to a gravel plain I could see his fort, a large square enclosure, of which the mud walls were ten feet high. To the right of the fort, behind a crumbling wall half buried in drifts of sand, was a garden of dusty, ragged palm-trees."

Today, tribal raids and high-sea piracy are a distant memory, having been replaced by more sophisticated means of international trade and consummate statecraft. This became patently necessary after the discovery of oil, when riches beyond the wildest dreams of local tribal chieftains brought the interest and involvement of the giants of the international petroleum industry to their shores.

The desert Bedu's diet of dates, milk and curd cheese was supplemented through the ages with birds and small mammals caught by trained falcons, notably the peregrine and saker. The birds were traditionally trapped during their autumn migration from the Russian Steppes to Africa and painstakingly trained by a handler with whom the birds lived. Most of the falcons were released after the hunting season, returning season after season, sometimes caught by the same handler.

When attacking, the falcon climbs high and dives at speeds of up to 305 kilometres per hour (180 miles per hour) – faster than any other bird – dispatching its unsuspecting prey in one fell swoop.

An icon of the Bedouin way of life, falcons can be seen in many old photographs of successive Sheikhs who harboured a passion for falconry. Sheikh Saeed Al Maktoum (Ruler of Dubai 1912 – 1958) loved the sport and flew his birds on the outskirts of Dubai where the *houbara* bustard was still abundant. His sons, Sheikh Rashid and Sheikh Khalifa, accompanied him when they came of age. Sheikh Saeed also went on hunting trips to the neighbouring Sheikhdom of Ras Al Khaimah, where the Al Maktoum family owned several date plantations.

Sheikh Rashid himself in turn took his own sons on hunting expeditions with falcon and rifle, visiting neighbouring countries in search of the *houbara* and gazelle. Today, the falcon is as important a part of Dubai's heritage as the horse and camel, symbolising a link to the past rooted in true desert traditions.

So close is the relationship still engendered amongst young and old that there is a fully-fledged falcon hospital in Dubai set up by the Ruling Family. The hospital caters to the veterinary needs of an increasing number of falconers that are breeding or importing birds from around the globe. It is just as well, for some birds imported from Europe, America or Central Asia can cost up to US$50,000 each.

The Dubai Crown Prince, Sheikh Mohammed bin Rashid Al Maktoum and his brother, Sheikh Hamdan, are very keen falconers themselves. Sheikh Mohammed is an avid hunter and travels widely in Southeast Asia in search of good falconry, and to the far corners of the globe in search of sporting trophies.

Men had to be resourceful and versatile, able to hunt as well as to fight. They had to handle horses and camels, tend to the palm groves and go fishing and pearling. While they were away, their women were responsible for raising the children, tending the animals and working the date palms, in addition to making and mending the material trappings of everyday life. Using mostly goat's hair, the women made rugs, tents, saddle-bags and accessories for camels and horses. Wool was combed on a board with protruding nails, then spun on a wooden hand-spindle. This thread was spun into a ball, which was then stretched on a ground loom for weaving.

Designs incorporated geometric patterns, such as stripes, squares, rectangles, diamonds and triangles. Brown, orange and cream dyes were produced locally by crushing plants found in the desert.

From this simple, utilitarian lifestyle were made the practical garments still worn today: *dishdasha* or *thobe* – long white cotton outer garment worn by men. *Abaya* or *bisht* – finely-woven black or gold cloak originally made of camel hair and worn over the *dishdasha* on special occasions, and black camel-hobble or material cord, *agal*, to secure the *gutra* – white headcloth. Under the *gutra* the men wore a lace skullcap – *gahfia* or *tagia*.

Women are clothed in a long black cloak, *abaya*, and black head cloth called a *shayla*. The more conservative also wear a *burqa*, a stiff mask of gold coloured material, covering the eyebrows, nose and mouth.

Henna is often used to decorate hands and feet. The green powder is derived from leaves of the henna tree, mixed with water to create a reddish-brown paste that is applied using a paper cone to squeeze the paste onto the skin, much like cake icing. After washing off the paste, the intricate patterns remain for up to six weeks.

Jewellery tended to be elaborate and heavy, and came in the form of head-dresses, necklaces, collars, anklets and bracelets. These sometimes incorporated semi-precious stones such as coral, amber, turquoise and carnelian as well as glass beads and cowry shells.

Silversmiths often used silver melted down from poor quality Maria Theresa dollars minted centuries before, but which were still legal tender in the region until the 1950s. Part of the bride-price paid by the groom was jewellery that remained the bride's own property – her personal, portable wealth in case of divorce or widowhood.

Beyond a few basic necessities and personal adornments, tribal cultivators and nomadic Bedu had little use for arts and elaborately decorative crafts. Language itself, and oral poetry in particular, became the living art form. Under vast desert skies, searingly hot by day and alive with the brilliance of the constellations at night, the men folk would weave tales of past events and dream of futures untold. Tales of chivalry, passages of history and the exploits of heroes became the language of shared interests and united common bonds.

Anyone who has sat with the Bedouin at night in the desert around a few charred acacia twigs glowing within a circle of weather-worn rocks will understand that story-telling is an art that casts a healing spell. As the bespeckled cloak of night is drawn across the firmament, the tilting coffee-pot replenishes endless cups of bitter, cardamom-flavoured coffee as men dream their dreams.

The Bedu have a saying that a story lies locked in each grain of desert sand. Tales reminiscent of *The Thousand and One Nights* or *The Arabian Nights* are told and retold to attentive, pensive ears. Collected between the eighth and fourteenth centuries, the traditional Arabian fables *Alf Layla wa-Layla*, tell of legendary ingenuity, courage and bravery – fabulous and fanciful tales anchored in everyday life. *The Arabian Nights* was introduced to Europe by Antoine Galland, whose *Mille et Une Nuits* was based on a Syrian manuscript first published in France between 1704 and 1717.

Verbal dexterity born of many such nights has created skilled negotiators and arbiters that have helped steer the Sheikhdom's destiny. Thesiger wrote: "All that is best in the Arabs has come to them from the desert: their religious instinct, which has found expression in Islam; their sense of fellowship, which binds them as members of one faith; their pride of race; their generosity and sense of hospitality; their dignity and the regard which they have for the dignity of others as fellow human beings; their humour, their courage and patience, the language which they speak and their passionate love of poetry."

LEFT
Women carried water drawn from the wells in semi-porous pots or jahala. As the water evaporated, it cooled the contents of the jars.

RIGHT
A local falconer and his bird, out of the pages of history.

DEVELOPING A NATION

*"An assemblage of mud hovels surrounded by a low mud wall in which are
several breaches, and defended by three round towers, and a square
castellated building, with a tower at one angle."*
(A report by British naval captain M. Houghton in 1822 describing Dubai)

By 1820 the area around the Creek had become a well-established fishing
and pearling community. Dubai's oldest surviving building, Al Fahidi fort
built in 1799, is probably the "square, castellated building" to which
Houghton referred. Forts were traditionally simple rectangles with guard
towers at each corner. Al Fahidi, on the Bur Dubai side of the Creek, was
used as the Ruler's residence and seat of government and as a shelter for
people in case of attack, as well as being the local jail.

In 1971, a multi-million dollar investment converted the fort into
Dubai Museum, depicting life in and around the town before the formation
of modern Dubai.

Smaller refuges were normally used by herdsmen and cultivators in
times of tribal feuds to defend against attack by hostile raiders. They were
constructed to protect wells or irrigation channels, palm groves and grazing
land. While the lower level was used to store grain, the facade was speckled
with narrow firing slits from which the occupants would scour the horizon
for intruders. Such elevated watch-towers can still be found dotted around
the Emirates.

The Rulers of the north-east wedge of the Arabian Peninsula
emerged from these challenging, character-forming cultures of the desert.
One tribe – the Bani Yas – was among the largest and most highly regarded
of southern Arabia, comprising some 20 subsections. Other tribes sought
protection under the wing of the Bani Yas's superior military prowess and
proven loyalty to their allies. Originally based in the Liwa oasis, the Al Bu
Falah subsection resettled in 1793 in Abu Dhabi, and annexed Dubai with
its population of 1,200 as a dependency. Sheikh Shakhbut of the Al Nahyan
branch of the Bani Yas assumed political power and his family have ruled
Abu Dhabi ever since.

In an effort to reduce tribal disputes and protect trade, the British
signed the General Treaty of Peace with the nine Rulers of the coastal
Sheikhdoms in 1820. This first in a series of truces with Britain outlawed
plunder, piracy and undeclared wars. The agreements generated a
collective name for the independent Sheikhdoms – the Trucial Coast –
forming the basis for the United Arab Emirates (UAE) 150 years later.

In 1833 some 800 members of the Al Bu Falah branch of the Bani
Yas migrated north to the fishing village of Bur Dubai, led jointly by Sheikh
Maktoum bin Buti and Sheikh Obaid bin Saeed bin Rashid, declaring the
town's independence from Abu Dhabi. Sheikh Obaid died of old age shortly
afterwards and Sheikh Maktoum bin Buti began the Al Maktoum family's
rule of Dubai. He consolidated power and by 1841 was extending his
influence to Deira, and later to Shindagha.

The origin of the name Dubai – Dibai or Dubayy – is uncertain.
Some attribute it to a combination of the Farsi words for two and brothers,
referring to Deira and Bur Dubai. Others say it was derived from the market
named Daba, or the spiny-tailed lizard, Dab, once found in these parts.
Or perhaps the affluent trading centre of Dubai took its name from the
word meaning money.

In the Perpetual Treaty of Peace made in 1853, the Sheikhs undertook
not to wage war against each other in return for British protection. Thus
the British became the self-proclaimed protectorate power of the southern

Gulf mini-States.

The 1892 Exclusive Agreement with Britain prohibited the Trucial Rulers from contact with representatives of any other foreign power. It was an agreement that was to be robustly tested when other nations began to smell the Gulf's oil.

During the nineteenth century Britain also imposed its values by helping to eliminate slavery from the coast. Yet, in Islamic society, slaves enjoyed a different status to that experienced under the rule of Western colonial powers. They had rights and were protected by law, while slave owners were bound by the Koran to treat them humanely. Nevertheless, any slave who sought the protection of the British Crown – symbolised by grasping the flagpole in the compound of the British Agency or Consulate – was made free and given a Certificate of Manumission.

Throughout this period, pearling continued to flourish. So much so that by the mid-nineteenth century some 22,000 people and 1,200 boats were engaged in pearling along the coast, including 335 boats operating from Dubai, one of which – a pearling *sambuk* – is currently on show in

Dubai Museum. The industry yielded annual revenues of £5,000 towards the end of the century, and pay for the individual workers was a share of the proceeds, making them literal slaves to fortune.

The economy and social life of old Dubai at the end of the nineteenth century was centred on the pearling industry. Pearling was a way of life and source of *baraka* – heavenly benevolence. Everything depended on the proceeds of the catch and the success of the pearling trips signalled the difference between life and death, as the income had to sustain the populace for the entire year.

Besides pearl dealing (*letwash*), Dubai's catalogue of thriving activities at the end of the nineteenth century included dhow building (*leglaf*), blacksmithing (*lehdad*) and an increasingly lucrative entrepôt trade.

At the turn of the twentieth century, the settlement was divided into three distinct areas: Deira was the largest and the main commercial centre. Bur Dubai and Shindagha on the western bank were separated by a wide stretch of sand that flooded during high tide. Shindagha – probably the site of the original Bani Yas village situated on a narrow strip of land

separating the sea from the Creek – was the smallest area and the main residential district where the ruling Sheikhs traditionally lived.

The vernacular style of architecture in Dubai is the result of a mixture of three dominant factors: a hot and humid climate, religion and customs of its people and locally available building materials.

A few surviving watch-towers, forts and wind-towers dominated the settlements. Most dwellings comprised simple huts made from split trunks and fronds of palm trees, with roofs of woven palm leaves. The floor was the brushed sand of the desert. These *barasti* houses were surrounded by palm frond fences forming a corral to protect the livestock at night.

A new window of opportunity for growth came unsolicited when the fortunes of Lingah on the Persian coast declined. At the time, Lingah was the dominant port near the Straits of Hormuz and was controlled by Arab-speaking tribes. The Imperial Iranian Government abolished Lingah's Arab governorship, and took over administration in 1902, appointing the Imperial Bank of Iran to collect custom duties on their behalf.

With the imposition of Persian custom duties, trade was unsurprisingly driven away and Dubai prospered as a result. Many merchants moved across the Gulf, returning home to the 'City of Merchants'. In 1901 Sheikh Maktoum bin Hasher Al Maktoum, father of Sheikh Saeed and grandfather of Sheikh Rashid, paved the way for the move by abolishing import and export tariffs and establishing Dubai as a free trade port. He also began a systematic programme to encourage Lingah's leading merchants to relocate to Dubai by offering free land and personal guarantees of protection, swelling Dubai's population to 10,000 by 1908. Dubai's major trading families became powerful and influential members of society.

The immigrants from the district of Bastak in Fars near the port of Khamir, and other Iranian provinces settled in an area of Dubai to the east of Al Fahidi Fort that became known as Bastakia. They chose a location close to the Creek and near the souk because their livelihoods were based on trade, and this was a convenient point for off-loading their boats.

The Creek provided a vibrant artery into the lungs of the community, reaching nine miles into the desert. It had been the magnet for trading dhows throughout the centuries and from 1903 onwards began to receive ships from the British Indian Steam Navigation Company.

Until a major fire in 1894 destroyed many of the dwellings in Deira, most of the houses were made of palm fronds. The inferno triggered a new phase of development. While lower income inhabitants continued to live in the palm frond *barasti* houses well into the mid-twentieth century, the richer families began constructing dwellings from coral, stone and gypsum.

Gypsum was dug out of the salt marshes at the end of the Creek and baked, while coral-stone was lifted from the shallow waters of the Creek. The more substantial rafters that are often seen protruding untidily from external walls were made of date palm trunks or the more durable mangrove poles (*chandals*) imported from Africa. The rafters were then covered with palm-leaf matting and gypsum.

In summer the heat reaches intolerable levels, especially near the more humid coast. An ingenious method of catching and channelling even the mildest breeze was brought across the Gulf by fabric and pearl traders from Bastak in Persia (southern Iran) when they settled in Dubai in the early 1900s. The Bastakia district of Dubai still displays a concentration of some 50 wind-tower houses, restored by the municipality in the 1990s using traditional techniques.

Badgeer or *badgir* in Persian means 'wind-catcher', and translates to *barjeel* or *barajil* in Arabic and wind-tower in English. Earliest towers were made of sackcloth or cotton, and were superimposed on traditional palm frond huts. Screens of canvas sailcloth were arranged crosswise as scoops to channel air directly down into the house through material soaked in water, thus cooling the air. Matting flaps or vents regulated the flow, while allowing hot air to rise and escape.

The square wind-towers have four open sides, each of which is hollowed into a concave V-shape, which traps the wind from any direction and deflects it downwards, cooling the rooms below. Water thrown on the floor beneath the tower cools the house as it evaporates.

This natural and energy-saving form of air-conditioning spread throughout the Gulf and has been incorporated into Dubai's modern architecture. Later wind-towers were made of alabaster, often ornamented with ceramic decorations.

In a further attempt to reduce the stifling summer heat, houses were constructed close to each other with narrow alleys (*sikkas*) between them from north to south, ending at the Creek.

Wealthy traders lived in large houses with decorative doorways leading into the inner courtyard, always the heart of the household. This courtyard-cum-garden provided light and shade with the fresh cooling air

In the heat of the day a young man in charge of his father's shop in the souk takes a break. Until the mid-twentieth century most of the buildings were made of palm fronds. This Old Dubai Souk image is a far cry from the plush and exotic souks and shopping malls that are a featured attraction for any visitor to the Emirate.

generated by plants and trees surrounded by rooms and balconies, with roofs and ceilings made of hardwoods brought in dhows from Zanzibar on the East African coast.

In deference to Islamic rules of privacy and modesty, the rooms were open to the courtyard but the exterior walls had few windows, just ventilation shafts positioned near the ceilings. The decorative element in the doors has regional and Indian influences, and one of the most charming aspects of vernacular architecture of Dubai are the old doors that you can still come across in the Bastakia district.

Every house or tent had a segregated area called the *harim*, including the courtyard, kitchen and separate rooms for the exclusive use of the women and children. The *harim* was intended to protect women from intrusive outside male eyes. This extended protection and enforced modesty applies equally outside the home, where women wear clothing to mask and veil themselves – the mask (*burqa*), veil (*shayla*) and the black overall coat (*abaya*).

Typical of the architecture of this time, but on a larger scale, is Sheikh Saeed Al Maktoum's house by the Creek in Shindagha. Built in 1896, it shows living quarters arranged around the courtyard with teak doors, wooden lattice screens and balustrades fortified by four wind-towers.

Above the entrance to one of the rooms was a sign that read: "Oh house, let no grief enter you and let not the time betray your owner."

The 30-room house served for many years as the residence of several generations of the Al Maktoum family living in separate apartments. It was Sheikh Saeed's home until his death in 1958.

The house re-opened in 1986 as a museum to commemorate pre-oil days, incorporating the social, cultural, educational and religious history of the Emirate, including a model of Bur Dubai in the 1950s that illustrates the striking contrast to the city of today.

Some of the windows in the wealthier residences were half-moon shaped and made of alabaster. Chinks were cut in ornate floral patterns to keep out harsh light but let in the cooling breeze. Carved wooden doors in forts and private houses included abstract stellar or floral motifs, often with a verse of classical Arabic prose from the Koran on the lintel. Ornate doors were mostly imported from India and many owners took the doors with them when they moved.

Wilfred Thesiger described Dubai in 1949: "Rowing boats patrolled the Creek to pick up passengers from the mouths of alleys between the high coral houses, surmounted with square wind turrets and pleasingly decorated with plaster moulding. Behind the diversity of houses which line the waterfront were the *souqs*, covered passageways where merchants sat cross-legged in the gloomy narrow alcoves among their piled merchandise.

"The *souqs* were crowded with many races – pallid Arab townsmen, armed bedu, quick-eye and imperious, Negro slaves, Baluchis, Persians and Indians. Among them I noticed a group of Kashgai tribesmen in their distinctive felt caps, and some of the Somalis off a *sambuk* from Aden."

By the mid-twentieth century, souks were busy with trade in imported rice, sugar, coffee, flour and animal ghee; while charcoal, fresh produce and livestock were transported from the interior. There were separate souks for pearls, spices, jewellery, foodstuffs and textiles.

In Deira's Old Souk, shops selling similar goods were grouped together – rice and pulses, textiles and clothing, stationery. The Spice Souk was a feast for the olfactory senses, especially the amber chunks of sweet-smelling frankincense. Some sense of those times is recreated in the present spice market where one can walk through a kaleidoscope of colours and smells.

The Souk Al Banian quarter next to the Dubai Souk was a focal point for Hindus and other Indians. Dubai Rulers and merchants encouraged Indian merchants to come and invest in local trade. Indians traded in perfumes, herbs and spices, silks and cotton cloth, tinned produce, sugar in solid cones, metals and manufactured goods such as rifles and cooking pots.

The Indian rupee was accepted as the currency during the period of British control of India. From 1948 until the formation of the UAE in 1971, the Gulf rupee was legal tender, while Maria Theresa silver dollars, called *riyals*, were also minted until 1950, still bearing the date 1780.

The entrance into Deira's covered Gold Souk, probably the largest in Arabia, is through a large wooden door on Sikkat Al Khail Street. Although prices are linked to the international daily gold rate, Dubai has acquired the name 'City of Gold'. Less than half of the gold jewellery is made in Dubai, the rest being imported from such diverse places as India, Saudi Arabia, Bahrain, Kuwait, Turkey, Singapore and Italy.

Many Indians resident in Dubai were goldsmiths, and large quantities of gold were supplied to India where its price was fixed at a higher rate than on the prevailing free market. The absence of customs duties facilitated Dubai's role as an important transhipment centre, and the unfettered

PRECEEDING PAGE
Looking up from inside the base of a wind-tower, similar to ones built in the early 1900s.

Until formal education began in Dubai in 1956, children were taught to read and write in mosque schools that focused on religious teaching and study of the Koran. Learning was mostly by rote and by copying written texts.

movement of gold became crucial to Dubai's economy. Contraband shipments of gold to the Indian subcontinent were the most important contributors to the coffers of the coastal Sheikhdoms before the advent of oil. With the completion of the dredging of the Creek in 1959, gold smuggling rose dramatically, peaking in 1970 at 259 tons of gold passing through Dubai en route to India.

In the 1950s the Dubai Souk extended 200 metres along the waterfront. Narrow lanes were roofed with matting and the sun streaked down through slits in the canopy along sombre tunnels lined with small cell-like shops.

The souks were alive with Bedu tradesmen carrying camel sticks, Omani merchants in their high-necked dishdashas, solemn Somali tribesmen and Kashgai nomads from the Zagros Mountains in Iran. Wealthy Persian merchants with long, flowing robes and gold-brocaded head-dresses wandered among industrious artisans – blacksmiths, carpenters, cobblers, tailors, goldsmiths and potters, each grouped together giving every section of the souk its own distinctive sounds and smells. The hammering of smiths,

scent of carpenters' sandalwood, the rhythmic clicking of tailors' sewing machines made up the clamour of an Eastern market place.

Shopping was itself a dignified ritual. Customers were offered a seat on a rug or stool, while coffee, tea or cold drinks were served. Earnest discussions took place about quality and price. Today, these age-old traditions are kept alive, even in the modern shopping malls where bargaining over prices can be overheard in every shop or stall.

While Hindu merchants were settling in Dubai, a substantial and prosperous Gulf Arab community was established in Bombay. Arab pearl dealers and other traders were exposed to Bombay's more advanced schools, hospitals, telegraph and post offices, and it was these traders who became Dubai's latter-day modernisers, fostering the growth of new skills and ideas.

The Al Ahmadiya School in Dubai was the first to be established in the region, endowed by a philanthropic pearl merchant and businessman named Ahmed bin Dalmouk. The school provided the first rung on the local education ladder for most of the Emirate's leading figures who were taught by rote.

The school was built in Ras Deira in 1912 and adopted religious teaching as the basis for education, with Arabic grammar, English, mathematics, geography and history also on the curriculum. Like most buildings from the era, a decorative doorway opened into the courtyard (*al housh*) surrounded by verandahs (*iwans*) leading to various rooms. In the courtyard, the pupils did their exercises, recited poetry, enjoyed their breaks and took part in events.

What is now Heritage House was the residence of Ahmed bin Dalmouk from 1910, and a nearby mosque and street are named after him. Built in 1890, Heritage House was bought by the Dubai Municipality in 1993 and renovated using traditional methods.

Ahmed bin Dalmouk was a leading trader and philanthropist. The first car ever imported into Dubai belonged to Ahmed, who made a gift of it to the Ruler Sheikh Saeed bin Maktoum.

Formal modern education began in Dubai in 1956 when the Al Ahmadiya School introduced a new curriculum with subjects such as English, Sociology and Science. By 2002 Dubai had 89 formal education schools, and the Information Technology Academy created by Sheikh Mohammed bin Rashid Al Maktoum to furnish all schools and colleges with advanced computer technology.

With trade flourishing at the beginning of the twentieth century, many mosques were built in residential and commercial districts by local merchants and religious benefactors. Until the early 1960s, most students had received their education through religious teachings while studying the Koran at such mosque schools, which also taught Arabic and maths. As in many cultures where children are expected to help supplement family incomes, there was often conflict between studies and the need for children to help with household chores, dhow building or pearl diving.

Pearl trading, which had reached its peak at the turn of the twentieth century, suddenly collapsed in the late 1920s. Ironically, the year preceding the collapse had been misleadingly prosperous. People over-extended themselves by taking out loans with high annual rates of interest of up to 36 per cent in order to buy new boats in search of the ever-more elusive pearl.

The Wall Street crash of 1929 and subsequent economic recession compounded the problems, with pearls losing their lustre in the capital cities of the Western world. The final death knell was sounded by the invention of the cultured pearl in Japan. Connoisseurs knew that cultured pearls could never match the exquisite nature of their natural counterparts, but the price of pearls tumbled nevertheless.

A way of life for an entire people was destroyed. Boat captains went bankrupt, divers sank deeper into debt and merchants had to fall back on less lucrative trade. Poverty, grinding hardship and malnutrition brought many households to their knees. Infant mortality was high and malaria became endemic.

It was one of the region's darkest hours. People had to find new opportunities to adopt and adapt.

Although natural pearls are no longer harvested from the Gulf, Hassan Al Fardan, a world authority on the Gulf pearl and a leading pearl dealer himself, remembers with deep nostalgia the times of his father and grandfather. "Pearls are my passion," he confides as he handles his huge collection, while singing and talking to the pearls. "Even before oil, this country was rich. Pearls were exported to India and China and my grandfather exported pearls to Baghdad. Although cultured pearls are now nearing natural pearls in terms of quality, for me they will always be dead pieces. Today, my market is in the UAE. There are plenty of people here who want to buy the natural pearl."

The late Sultan Al Owais, one of Dubai's leading traders and principal pearl merchants, owned the largest private pearl collection in the world, which is now displayed on the top floor of the National Bank of Dubai's modernistic high-rise headquarters overlooking the Creek.

Born in 1878, Sheikh Saeed bin Maktoum Al Maktoum began his 46-year rule in 1912 when pearling was still thriving, and Dubai was developing as one of the Gulf's leading ports. An unimposing man, he drew his strength from the traditions of desert survival and was guided by the teachings of Islam. Steering Dubai through the most turbulent of times and ruling with vision and authority, he continued his father's open door policy of welcoming merchants from southern Persian ports to settle in Dubai with their families.

At the time, Al Furda, the old customs house at the mouth of the Creek doubled as the Ruler's Office. Further up the Creek, the Emiri Diwan or Ruler's Court, served as Dubai's seat of government.

Sheikh Saeed held his daily *majlis* – informal discussions open to all citizens without restriction – at this spot. This tradition is still maintained today by the Sheikhs, despite increasingly busy schedules. The majlis is usually a comfortable, cushioned meeting place or reception area, an open forum in which to discuss proposals or air disputes about anything and everything, from disputed ownership of camels to land claims, from trade arbitration to family feuds. Sheikh Saeed and his brother Sheikh Hashar frequently acted as arbiters, settling disputes between merchants, and listening to citizens' complaints and suggestions.

His summer retreat – Majlis Ghorfat Um Al Sheef, also known as Majlis Al Ghoraifa – was built in 1955. A two-storey meeting place with verandas, teak doors and windows, it served as a police station in the 1960s, but has since been restored to its former state with the addition of a *falaj* irrigation system in the gardens.

Sheikh Rashid bin Saeed Al Maktoum was born in 1906. He was educated at the Al Ahmadiya School in Deira, where his lessons included Islamic studies, Arabic and arithmetic.

Sheikh Rashid's mother, Shaikha Hissah bint Al Mur Umm Rashid, was a strong character and wielded much influence during the first half of the twentieth century, helping to mould her son's character. She taught him to be involved in and maintain control over different affairs in Dubai. His astute mind was more than a match for the locals, and the British often came off the worst when they tried to manipulate affairs to their own advantage.

Both Sheikh Saeed and Sheikh Rashid have entered the history books as two of the most forward-thinking leaders along the Trucial Coast. Sheikh Rashid's *majlis* was described as 'an Arabian Camelot', a creative environment in which people were allowed to speak freely with no restrictions on what could be said. This cultivated an atmosphere of open debate, providing a nursery for innovative ideas and a forum in which people were challenged to think and perform beyond cultural or self-imposed limitations.

In a foreword to a book on Sheikh Rashid, Sheikh Hamdan bin Rashid Al Maktoum, UAE Minister of Finance and Industry and Deputy Ruler of Dubai, writes of his father: "My father believed that progress should benefit all, and made it his life's mission to spread those benefits as widely as he could. His humility was one of the most striking traits of my father's character, and the one which helped him maintain his common touch even when he was rubbing shoulders with world leaders and affecting the course of history. Throughout his life, my brothers and I watched him deal with

presidents and paupers with equal dignity and humanity."

Hamad bin Sukat, a close friend of Sheikh Rashid, wrote of him: "He was hungry to develop Dubai from its basic level. Sheikh Saeed had learned to rely on his son's good judgement. When something had to be done, Sheikh Rashid did the job. He liked to build and create. He had a natural authority and used it."

By 1939 the population of Dubai had increased to 20,000. During the 1930s and 1940s Dubai had become a criss-cross maze of narrow streets and tiny alleyways. At night, kerosene lamps hissed in front of the more prosperous houses. Night watchmen each looked after 10 to 12 shops by making their rounds, rattling drawn shutters to ensure they were properly locked. The crime rate was low and strict religious punishments ensured an orderly regime.

Life for many presented few opportunities beyond the perpetual round of prayers and meagre meals as they watched the world go by. Both men and boys shaved their heads and allowed their beards to grow. People lived on a diet of dates, fish, beans and peas supplemented by bananas, tomatoes and almonds imported from India. The almonds were a particular delicacy, pounded into a paste to provide a nutritious snack.

These were times when swarms of locusts brought annually devastating infestations. The coast was a potent breeding ground for this pest, as swarms travelled 160 kilometres (100 miles) a day, each locust eating the equivalent of its own weight.

The Gulf has always been reverentially referred to by local sailors and fishermen alike as 'the Big Sea'. It was, after all, their lifeline and provided their livelihood.

Tidal shallows along the coast made fertile fishing grounds, ideal for traps or cast nets. In V-shaped traps – *hadra* – fish were channelled along a stake-fence into a small enclosure that was harvested at low tide. Small, mobile traps – *garghour* – made of woven palm fronds and weighed down by stones, baited to entice fish through a narrow opening from which they found it difficult to escape. Dried *doma,* small sardine-like fish that were plentiful in these waters, were fed to cows or used as fertiliser.

The Sheikhs kept their armed retainers well into the twentieth century and, until the 1940s, the whole region was largely untamed. Sheikh Rashid, a warrior himself in his younger days, fought to secure his father's territories and to put down lawless tribal groups. The Awamir tribe was particularly powerful and virtually independent of any outside control. They constantly attacked small towns, stealing cattle, goats and produce. Sheikh Rashid and Sheikh Zayed bin Sultan Al Nahayan of Abu Dhabi decided to put a stop to this lawlessness and mounted joint desert attacks, driving the Awamir out of their area.

During these harsh times in the late 1930s and early 1940s, known as *seneen al qahat* or the years of drought, sanitation and medical care were non-existent. As greater demands were made on well water-tables, they became polluted by salt water and the drinking water had to be carried into town in four-gallon cans on the backs of donkeys.

Following the outbreak of World War II, the influence of the wider world began to penetrate into the fabric of life in Dubai. Having been an important commercial staging post en route to India, Dubai now became a strategic military enclave as Britain needed more operational bases in the Gulf.

The British decided to depose the regime in Iran and imposed an economic embargo by banning food imports to Iran's southern ports. They subsequently restricted the import of foodstuffs to Dubai. In an astute political move redolent of his diplomatic cunning, Sheikh Rashid promised to organise the controlled imports himself. He appointed a number of merchants in the Dubai Souk to sell food – rice, sugar, tea and flour – through a system of ration cards that were issued at the Ruler's Office (Emiri Diwan) signed by himself.

Imports were supervised by the British authorities and delivered to the Dubai Government, who in turn distributed the supplies to the appointed merchants. In most cases the ration quotas exceeded the needs of local families, who were then free to sell the surplus at very high prices to traders smuggling the food into Iran. The scheme guaranteed food to the people of Dubai, whilst giving them the opportunity to profit from the sale of surpluses.

Following the end of the second world war, Britain withdrew from India in 1947 and no longer had a need to maintain its strategic influence in the area, but it would be two decades before the British finally pulled out politically and militarily from the Gulf.

As late as 1948, when Dubai and Sharjah were the largest trading centres in the region, Abu Dhabi was still little more than a fort with 100 or so *barasti* (palm frond) huts and a few crumbling houses of coral-stone and gypsum.

It was around this time that a young British political agent, Ronald Codrai, arrived to work in the oil fields of Dubai, reminiscing in his memoirs written many years later: "there were no roads, no telephones, no electricity, no medical or other services, and along the coast every single drop of sweet water had to be hauled from hand-dug wells. There were no formal frontiers between the states, and no security, levy or police force other than the small number of armed tribesmen retained by each of the ruling Sheikhs. It was a strongly tribal society, and outside the main centres it was rare to meet anyone who was not armed with a rifle, a bandolier and the *khanjar* – the distinctive curved dagger of southern Arabia."

Prior to the introduction of electricity in the 1950s, kerosene lamps or candles were used for lighting. Charcoal, imported from the interior of Oman, was used for cooking and making coffee, and sweet water was then still available from wells around Dubai. It was a life of few luxuries, austere and simple, yet rich with dignity.

Despite the demise of the pearling industry, trade continued to thrive and the Gulf boasted the largest merchant sailing fleet in the world in terms of numbers of vessels, not in tonnage.

The word 'dhow', once used only by foreigners, is believed to have come from the Swahili *dau*. The design blueprint is reminiscent of the early Portuguese trading vessels, but the boats came in several variations – *al booms, sambuks, jaulbauts, baghalas, qutiyahs* and the thin, high-prowed *shahuf* – all now collectively known as dhows. *Al boom* was the largest of the dhows, and has more recently given its name to the Al Boom Tourist Village next to Al Garhoud Bridge on the Bur Dubai side of the Creek.

Dhow building skills have been retained despite the advent of modern materials such as fibreglass. The Rulers have stepped in to ensure that their heritage is both protected and promoted.

With no detailed plans, dhow builders – *qalaleef* – traditionally from the Indian subcontinent, design and construct their vessels by eye and a little help from rough sketches. The wood was imported from East Africa or the Malabar Coast in India, ropes from Zanzibar and sail canvas from Bahrain or Kuwait. Dhows that used to average about 23m in length are now 44m long and can travel at 13 knots carrying 900 tons of cargo, and they last for a 100 years.

Today, as dhows glide majestically up and down the Creek, small flat-decked, motorised water taxis – *abras* – shuttle back and forth

For centuries vessels from Dubai have carried cargo throughout the region and members of the crew have climbed mast and rigging with the dexterity of those adept at climbing palm trees. Today, marine engines have reduced the need for a large crew of agile sailors, and replaced the inspiring sight of billowing sails straining in the trade winds.

between them in a constant ebb and flow, carrying commuters, shoppers and tourists.

Trade – Dubai's early lifeline – remains the most important source of revenue today. In the unfolding story of Dubai's trade, the Creek has retained an importance as the focus of city life and the wharfs are used to transfer small and medium weight goods, but larger cargo and heavy industry had to look to new sites with enough space to develop the scope for modern facilities.

Good fortune lay in wait through developments beyond Dubai's shores. Oil was discovered in Persia (Iran) in 1908, sparking great international interest amongst Western governments and their respective oil companies for prospecting in Arabia and the Gulf. The region's first Arab oil was extracted in commercial quantities in Bahrain in 1932. Dubai's turn would come, heralding the beginning of phenomenal change.

Between 1935 and 1952, the Trucial Sheikhs – led by Sheikh Saeed bin Maktoum – signed concessions with the Iraq Petroleum Company, a London-based international consortium in which Britain had the controlling interest.

Dubai's oil wealth proved insufficient to allow complacency, but it did provide a catalyst for the development of a wide range of commercial and industrial enterprises, as well as funding sweeping infrastructure and social programmes.

The region that is now Dubai has survived for centuries by making the most out of very few resources, consciously broadening its economic base in order to avoid being left hostage to a single source of livelihood – be it fish, pearls or oil.

Sheikh Rashid's vision to build Dubai into a prosperous trading hub had been acutely frustrated by lack of finances. The beginning of the oil era set the scene for a new beginning in the history of this Sheikhdom.

A NEW MOMENTUM

"I remember the past when we had little, but we believed in God, loved our country and were faithful to our people. God has helped us to develop our country, to promote trade movement and remove all the obstacles that obstruct its progress, to enable trade to grow and to bring about prosperity and welfare. We shall continue to work in order to achieve the total success of trade in this country and for the benefit of the whole region. We will lay down better living conditions for our people and have made a start to boost construction activities and provide the necessary vital services."
(Sheikh Rashid bin Saeed Al Maktoum, in a 1969 press briefing)

Black tar seepages have for millennia found their way to the surface of the desert through the earth's geological cracks and fissures. The substance had proved most useful through time in providing an effective coagulant for wounds, the treatment of cataracts, toothaches, coughs, rheumatism and fever. Boat builders have for centuries caulked or waterproofed the timbers of their vessels with the oily substance.

No special interest was ever paid by the locals to the sticky black substance oozing from inside the earth. It must have been hard to imagine how this hidden gift of the gods could be more beneficial. It was only at the dawn of the twentieth century that the true extent of its potential began to be recognised, as technology advanced and new uses were being found for the oil.

When oil exploration began in the Trucial States, Sheikh Saeed and his son Sheikh Rashid were quick to appreciate the likely benefits and to take advantage of the opportunity presented them.

The Petroleum Concessions Ltd, a wholly-owned subsidiary of the Iraq Petroleum Company, was formed in 1935 and the Dubai government was the first to grant concessions to this company in 1937 in return for modest payments and an annual rent.

The Superior Oil Company of America approached Dubai in the late 1930s, and again after the Second World War. But the British, citing the Exclusive Agreement of 1892, rejected advances made by other countries, nationals and companies despite the fact that the British were not themselves eager to develop the area's resource until such time as world demand grew more significantly. They jealously guarded their interests and bided their time.

Nevertheless, Superior Oil carried out an aerial survey of the marine areas of both Dubai and Abu Dhabi. The British considered their rights over the areas had been infringed and the British Government sued Superior Oil in the International Court of Justice at The Hague and won.

After much political wrangling, Abu Dhabi finally went with British Petroleum and Dubai signed an agreement with Continental Oil. As part of its policy intended to protect the interests of its people, the Dubai Government insisted on the employment of its own subjects in the oil industry after an initial period of training.

Although the war temporarily suspended oil exploration, Saudi Arabia and Kuwait's immense reserves of fossil hydrocarbons came on stream in the late 1940s. But Dubai's first well sunk in 1950 at Jebel Ali proved dry and was abandoned at over 3,660 metres (12,000 feet). Yet it was ultimately Dubai that spearheaded change in the oil producer governments' dealings with the international oil giants, by setting a precedent for the Trucial Coast when they first secured a 50:50 revenue sharing arrangement with the oil companies from their oilfields.

Long-standing local rivalries over the strategic value of hitherto empty desert land inevitably boiled over. This led to a three-year war of demarcation between Abu Dhabi and Dubai starting in 1945.

Sheikh Saeed's son, Sheikh Rashid, was at the time serving as Regent, assuming more and more state responsibilities. Bold and tireless, yet shy and subtle, Sheikh Rashid was a conservative man who warmed quickly to modern ideas. Tolerant and modest, he could be aggressive and ruthless in the interests of Dubai, never flinching from difficult decisions.

Sheikh Rashid's combination of leadership, judgement and determination gave considerable momentum to progress in the region. As a force for reconciliation, he resolved inter-tribal problems in the manner of a benevolent father working for the best interests of those concerned.

Sheikh Rashid had a massive job on his hands when he began to formulate plans for the future of Dubai. He started in the 1950s by bringing together the most talented individuals in the community and from elsewhere – bankers, builders, merchants and thinkers – to begin the daunting task of building a modern Emirate and fashioning his dream for the future of Dubai.

In his grand schemes, Sheikh Rashid also brought to play the talents of his sons Sheikh Mohammed, Sheikh Hamdan and Sheikh Maktoum, prescience rewarded by the role these three brothers have had in the transformation of Dubai in the decade since the death of their father.

When Sheikh Rashid seriously began to embark on this dream, the first building blocks for future growth had only recently been laid. Dubai's first bank had opened in 1946 – a branch of the Imperial Bank of Iran, predecessor to the British Bank of the Middle East (BBME). Prior to this, merchants kept their cash in iron boxes, and therefore welcomed the security of a bank in which to store surplus capital.

The absence of modern medicine was pronounced, with people still looking to traditional remedies and consulting knowledgeable old women or *mutawwa* (religious men). Access to modern medicine involved a long boat trip to India. In 1950 the first hospital on the Trucial Coast – the Maktoum Hospital – was established in Dubai with 38 beds, growing to 106 by 1968. The needs of the ever-expanding population were met by building the 200-bed Rashid Hospital that opened in 1972, and then the 635-bed Dubai Hospital in 1983.

Half a century after the establishment of the first hospital, medical facilities in Dubai are among the most advanced in the world, with state-of-the-art diagnostic, curative and preventive systems.

The health of the general populace began to improve gradually during the 1950s. Improved hygiene brought on by the provision of fresh water and sanitation, better diets and the extensive development of desert agri-business brought fresh produce to the majority of the people.

Meanwhile, the rise of Arab Nationalism was sweeping through the region, providing both a common identity for people who spoke Arabic as their native tongue and unsettling traditional regimes. At the initiative of British politician Anthony Eden, the Arab League was founded in 1945 to further co-operation between Arab states. But within a few years the Arab League, spurred on by Nasserism, was speaking out against British colonialism.

FAR LEFT
Shifting sands constantly silted up the entrance to Dubai Creek until a series of improvements during the 1950s helped ensure that this vital artery of trade was functioning efficiently throughout the year. This image shows Dubai in the 1930s.

LEFT
Sandbanks in the Creek, wind-tower houses and palm frond enclosures of Dubai city in the 1950s present a remarkable contrast to present day images, highlighting the phenomenal change that has taken place within living memory.

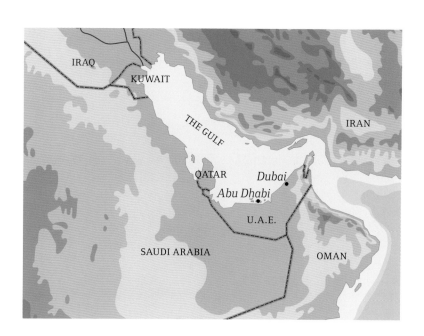

The Trucial States Council, set up in 1952, marked the first concerted attempt to bring some unity to the Sheikhdoms along the coastline of the Arabian Gulf. The Council provided a forum in which the Rulers of the Trucial Coast could assume greater control over the management of their own affairs, and served to lay the foundations for the establishment of the United Arab Emirates (UAE) in 1971. This informal body met twice a year under the initial Chairmanship of the British Political Agent in Dubai.

Though Dubai Creek had been improved in 1948, the shifting sandbanks and silting of the entrance began to hamper shipping and trade. It was against this background that the dredging of the Creek began in 1954 under the supervision of Sheikh Rashid with the encouragement of the British. A British firm of consultants, Sir William Halcrow and Partners, were asked to advise on the project, and Creek Bonds were sold to merchants to pay for the initial survey.

Considerable blasting, dredging, building of training walls and steel piling was needed to keep the channel free from silt. To help meet the costs, Sheikh Rashid hit upon an ingenious idea: materials taken from the Creek were dumped in the lower-lying areas, creating reclaimed sites suitable for sale as building land. The dredging was completed in 1959 and enabled the merchants of Dubai to compete effectively with their richer counterparts in Kuwait and Bahrain.

By the time Sheikh Rashid succeeded his father on his death in 1958, the kernels of the dream were beginning to take shape in Dubai. His eldest son, Sheikh Maktoum, was proclaimed Crown Prince and addressed the people for the first time on behalf of his father.

During the early 1960s, Sheikh Maktoum completed his local schooling, continuing his university education in Britain.

Sheikh Mohammed, Sheikh Rashid's third son, also began his formal education at the Al Ahmadiya School in 1955 before moving on to England in 1966 to study languages in Cambridge, there meeting a wide range of people in a melting pot of nationalities and cultures.

Dubai's population had reached 30,000 by 1956, tripling in less than fifty years. Such rapid growth needed management and planning.

Throughout the late 1950s and the early 1960s, Sheikh Rashid and his sons worked tirelessly to realise the dream of a developing Dubai. Maintaining the attitude of mind of a merchant prince, Sheikh Rashid was determined to create conditions in which trade would flourish, and focused on giving Dubai a broad economic foundation belying its oil-dependent culture, a trap many oil-based regional economies have not escaped.

Projects included the installation of electricity, the development of fresh water resources through huge desalination plants, building Dubai Airport as an international transit route and the construction of Dubai's first hotel. Schools and modern residential districts began to sprout up almost overnight.

Graeme Wilson writes in his book *Father of Dubai*: "Sheikh Rashid was adamant that the new breed of civil servants and technocrats should not stifle a mood of unbridled optimism which was attracting money and trade."

Dubai's momentum was gathering pace and Sheikh Rashid strove to remove stumbling blocks in order to facilitate progress. In 1958 he took up the issue of public electricity with the British Bank of the Middle East (BBME). The Dubai Electricity Company was inaugurated the following year and the Sheikhdom had its first city-wide electricity service in 1961.

By tapping local Bedouin knowledge of the desert, Sheikh Rashid ascertained that good water supplies could be obtained at Al Aweer. The Qatar Water Supply Company was employed in 1962 to start excavating in Al Aweer, and within two years water tanks had been built in Dubai to supply the city.

When finances would not permit, Sheikh Rashid himself would contribute personal funds to accelerate progress and development. Always prescient, he contributed over £30,000 in 1961 to establish a Dubai Trade School in Deira that opened its doors in 1964 with an initial intake of 36 local students.

Prior to the formation of the UAE, the education system had been based on the Kuwaiti model divided into four years of elementary, four of intermediate and four of secondary education. Kuwait used to supply Dubai's schools with books, teachers and funds.

In the 1960s Sheikh Rashid turned to Cairo for teachers to launch an extensive education programme. The Egyptian model with six years of elementary education, three of preparatory and three years of secondary education was adopted during the 1970s, although in 1971 students wishing to go beyond secondary education were financed by the Government to go abroad, usually to England or the USA.

Dubai needed a modern police force to replace the old system of civilian night watchmen and the Ruler's guards. Since 1951, it was the task

FAR LEFT
H.H. Sheikh Maktoum bin Rashid Al Maktoum, Ruler of Dubai, Prime Minister and Vice-President of the UAE.

TOP
H.H. Sheikh Hamdan bin Rashid Al Maktoum, Deputy Ruler of Dubai and UAE Minister of Finance.

LEFT
H.H. General Sheikh Mohammed bin Rashid Al Maktoum, Dubai Crown Prince and UAE Minister of Defence.

of Trucial Oman Scouts – formed at the behest of the Trucial States Council – to keep order and protect oil exploration in the interior. But in June 1956, the Dubai Police force was established in its place, accepting only citizens of the Trucial States and the Sultanate of Oman. By 1967 the force had expanded to 430 and in 1968, in his first public appointment the Ruler's third son, General Sheikh Mohammed bin Rashid Al Maktoum, presently both Crown Prince of Dubai and Minister of Defence of the UAE, was appointed Head of the Dubai Police and Public Security.

The Land Department was established in 1959 under the Chairmanship of Sheikh Rashid's eldest son, Sheikh Maktoum. Locals were encouraged to buy plots of residential land and given financial assistance to build housing. Families who had occupied land for generations with no formal documentation were encouraged to buy their plots.

Old Dubai residential districts were swiftly transformed, accommodating the Emirate's own burgeoning population as well as increasing numbers of expatriates who came to work in the Emirate, many of whom would later choose to base their regional headquarters in Dubai. Newly allocated funds were invested in construction that created a boom in the industry unlike any seen before in the region. For the first time merchants and traders could raise mortgages on property with documented proof of ownership. This frenetic construction activity continues apace, fuelling the booming economy and reinforcing Dubai's position as the centre of trade and commerce in the Gulf.

Vast schemes such as Palm Island and Dubai Marina are attracting greater numbers of outsiders to buy into Dubai's super-modern infrastructure for the first time, extending the depth of the economy and breadth of regional participation in its growth and prosperity. Ask any Middle East business person where they would ideally like to locate and Dubai crops up more than any other name.

From the establishment of the Dubai Municipality Council in its present form in 1961, it has been the Emirate's principal planning policy to provide housing for all nationals. Under the Chairmanship of Sheikh Hamdan bin Rashid Al Maktoum, Sheikh Rashid's second son and the UAE's Minister of Finance, the council has organised extensive and well-managed modern services within the urban area, including refuse collection, anti-malaria and pest control schemes, fire fighting and the provision of public gardens.

But Dubai was already on the move well before the advent of oil

revenues. In his Annual Report for 1962, the British Political Agent wrote: "Dubai's remarkable progress is unabated ... in Dubai, which is the centre from which the others take their pattern, the progressiveness of the Ruler effectively removes the sting from any complaints."

Yet in the early days of commercial aviation, Britain considered the neighbouring Sheikhdom of Sharjah to be the more important staging post en route to India. Although British Imperial Airways started to use Sharjah as a stopover in 1932, political manoeuvring resulted in the first military sea-plane landing on Dubai Creek in January 1934. From 1937, British Imperial Airways' flying boats used the Creek as a staging post between London, India and Australia, familiarising travellers en route with what was to become the leading regional airport of the future.

Dubai's first makeshift landing strip in the 1930s consisted of a 1,830 metre (6,000 feet) compacted sand runway near the old Deira graveyard, but Sheikh Saeed and his son Sheikh Rashid wanted a more substantial airport so that Dubai would not be disadvantaged by having to route part of its trade through Sharjah airport, especially when additional duty was imposed on all shipments arriving there by air.

During Sheikh Rashid's official visit to London in 1959, he held meetings with the British consulting group of International Aeradio, who confirmed the company's readiness to establish a landing strip and air traffic control system in Dubai.

Easa Saleh Al-Gurg, presently UAE ambassador to London at the Court of St James, was an advisor at the time to Sheikh Rashid and provides an interesting account in his autobiography of the ensuing events:

"One of the carriers of the weekly gold shipments was flown by an ex-RAF pilot named Freddie Bosworth. Sheikh Rashid realised that the inadequacy of Dubai's landing arrangements could not continue and we approached the Political Agent and argued the case for Dubai's need for its own airport, but he insisted that Sharjah would serve Dubai and other Sheikhdoms in its immediate vicinity.

"It was clearly time for some creative thinking. Sheikh Rashid instructed me to tell the leading merchants in the town to come to the Deira airstrip at 4.45 in the afternoon; Bosworth was also to be there with his aircraft ready for take-off. Finally, I was to ask the Political Agent to be there at 5.00pm. The merchants came and, with Sheikh Rashid and myself on board, Bosworth took off and flew down to the mouth of the Creek; as

we returned to the airstrip, on the way circling the Political Agency, we saw the Political Agent standing at the end of the makeshift runway. We flew down along the strip, dipped as we reached the end and then soared off again, all in the sight of the Political Agent who, by this time, must have wondered what was going on.

"As we landed Sheikh Rashid said to me, 'Easa, I am going to sacrifice you in the interests of Dubai. I shall say some very harsh things about you to the Political Agent when we land.'

"We hurried to where the Political Agent was standing, looking rather cross. 'Excellency,' said Sheikh Rashid, 'we waited for you. Whatever happened to you? Why did you not come with us?'

"Through clenched teeth the Political Agent explained that Easa Gurg had told him to come to the strip at 5.00pm.

"'That fool Easa Gurg,' said Sheikh Rashid. 'He can't get even the simplest message right.' He apologised most profusely to the Political Agent.

"The Political Agent still refused the request for an airport for Dubai, until Sheikh Rashid sent Bosworth to see the Political Resident, the Political Agent's superior official, and say that Dubai would bear the cost of the development and would not look to Britain to fund it. 'In that case,' said the Political Resident, 'you may certainly have your damn airstrip. In fact you may have ten airstrips if you want them.'"

Dubai International Airport (DIA) was thus born in 1959 and officially opened by Sheikh Rashid on 30th September 1960. Operations began with Heron and Dakota aircraft until a 9,200-foot asphalt runway was completed in 1965 to accommodate larger aircraft.

Meanwhile, Dubai's first bridge over the Creek – Al Maktoum Bridge – was opened to traffic in 1963, followed later by a road tunnel under the Creek near Shindagha and a second bridge – Al Garhoud – further inland. A third bridge is scheduled for completion in 2005.

By 1968 the Creek had developed to such an extent that the Ruler commissioned a development scheme for its entire nine-mile length, with financial assistance from Kuwait, Saudi Arabia and Qatar.

Transforming Dubai from a traditional culture to a sophisticated modern city required balancing vision with practical application. In order to manage the dramatic and rapid urban renewal, Sheikh Rashid continued his father's approach of personal involvement. His daily programme started after *fajr* (dawn) prayers when he made a tour of Dubai for about two hours

visiting projects under construction and dealing with problems on the spot. He was never satisfied with simple explanations, but wanted to have a detailed understanding of every stage of a project's progress. It is a family trait that is largely responsible for the Dubai success story, continuing to this day in the person of Sheikh Mohammed, who is often seen inspecting government offices, organisations and projects before the employees themselves arrive at work.

Sheikh Rashid would return home to his modest palace for half an hour's breakfast, then at about 7am went to his office for open meetings with businessmen, contractors, bankers, fishermen – anyone could approach his *majlis* to talk to him directly. He was extremely skilful at conducting negotiations and discussions without the formalities of portfolios or administrators that define ministers' roles in many other countries.

During Ramadan, Sheikh Rashid had a habit of staying up all night receiving people until the dawn prayers, and only then retiring.

Steeped in tradition, the Government of Dubai continues to be much closer to its people than many comparable systems. By adhering to the essence of Islamic culture and their Arab Bedu heritage, with free and unrestricted access to those in power, fewer tensions or grievances are allowed to accumulate.

There is a strong bond of trust between Rulers and officials, which facilitates efficient administration. The continuity of rule provided by a single family avoids the fragmented approach and short-term goals of governments seeking selective advantage to the detriment of medium and long-term national goals.

When the oil began to flow, the rules of life changed along with the tools of trade. Tens of thousands of expatriates came to work in Dubai, altering the population demographics forever. Cars began to replace camels, boats acquired motors, the pace of life quickened, commercial stakes increased and battles were fought using the tools of international business diplomacy. Protecting the indigenous population's interests is still paramount in the minds of its Rulers, but the well-being of over half a million foreign workers and the increasingly large numbers of international business people choosing Dubai as their operational base is a major consideration in the Dubai Government's planning and execution.

Dr Khalifa Mohammed Ahmed Suleiman, Chairman of the Ruler's Court and Chairman of the National Bank of Dubai, remembers Sheikh

FAR LEFT
Sheikh Hamdan presiding over a meeting of the Steering Committee of Dubai 2003, of which he is the Chairman. The Annual Meeting of the Board of Governors of the World Bank Group and the International Monetary Fund is being held for the first time in the Middle East in September 2003 in Dubai, highlighting the importance of the Emirate in the global financial community.

LEFT
Sheikh Mohammed with King Abdullah II of Jordan in Dubai, attending the Jordan Investment Conference in 2003. The Crown Prince of Dubai is not only the principal proponent for the Emirate's rapid development, but is also very active internationally in espousing the Arab cause on the world stage.

Rashid, "He was acutely aware that some other Gulf states had enveloped the business community in red tape, new taxes and stifling regulation. He often reminded those of us concerned with the commercial sector to make it as easy as possible for legitimate businesses to trade here. It was Sheikh Rashid's open door policy and a lack of red tape which attracted many to do business in Dubai."

The Trucial States Development Office was established in 1965 to manage the development of agriculture, health and technical education. The first project included a 13.5 kilometre surfaced road from Dubai to Sharjah and water and electricity supply schemes for all the state capitals.

As oil revenue began to pour into the neighbouring Sheikhdom of Abu Dhabi, its Ruler Sheikh Shakhbut found it impossible to adapt to the great change. In 1966 his popular younger brother, Sheikh Zayed bin Sultan Al Nahayan, was installed as the new Ruler of Abu Dhabi. The face of change was about to embrace the two neighbouring Sheikhdoms, with Dubai and Abu Dhabi leading the way towards modernisation within both the UAE and the entire region.

An ascetic figure, Bedu warrior, astute in negotiations and a skilled arbiter, Sheikh Zayed had a lively sense of humour and his generosity predated the gift of oil. He possessed great vision by moving to bury the enmities and jealousies of the past. Together with Sheikh Rashid, the two were largely instrumental in forging the union of the seven Emirates.

Four years after Abu Dhabi began to export oil, Dubai's offshore Fateh field was discovered in 1966 by the Dubai Marine Areas Company. Sheikh Rashid personally chose the name Fateh, meaning good fortune, and from the outset determined that oil income should be channelled into preparing Dubai for a time when oil production would decline.

Neither the largest nor richest of the Sheikhdoms in the region, Dubai continues to be a lynchpin in the successful modernising drive of the United Arab Emirates.

On 18th February 1968, Sheikh Rashid and Sheikh Zayed met at a desert camp on the Abu Dhabi-Dubai border. "So, Rashid, what do you think? Shall we create a union?" asked Sheikh Zayed. Without hesitation, the Dubai Ruler replied: "Give me your hand, Zayed. Let us shake upon an agreement. You will be President."

The signing of the union accord by Sheikh Rashid and Sheikh Zayed formed the kernel of the future federation. They then invited the

LEFT
H H Sheikh Rashid bin Saeed al Maktoum, the late Ruler of Dubai, with H H Sheikh Zayed bin Sultan Al Nahayan, President of the UAE and Ruler of Abu Dhabi. The two men were the decisive influence in forging the union of the seven Emirates into the United Arab Emirates in 1971.

RIGHT
The old Dubai International Airport was officially opened by Sheikh Rashid in 1960, when it handled Heron and Dakota aircraft.

FAR RIGHT
Heralding a new era of air transport, a military sea-plane landed on Dubai Creek in January 1934 and within three years, British Imperial Airways' flying boats regularly used the Creek as a staging post during their long journey between London, India and Australia.

other Trucial States, along with Qatar and Bahrain, to join a union that would jointly conduct foreign affairs, defence, security and social services, and adopt a common immigration policy. Nine Rulers met in Dubai for a constitutional conference and signed an agreement as an expression of intent to form a federation.

Bahrain, where oil had been discovered much earlier, was reluctant to rush into the federation. In the event, Bahrain and Qatar withdrew from the wider federal project. But the remaining seven states pursued the first Arab federal experiment that has succeeded beyond the imaginings of regional aspirants and international politicians. Though culturally more homogeneous, the seven Emirates vary considerably in size, resources and wealth.

Bringing some of the reluctant Sheikhs into the union and forging the blueprint for the future of the UAE required the wisdom of Sheikh Rashid and generosity and leadership of Sheikh Zayed, helping set aside previous periods of distrust and dissent. In this endeavour, they were ably assisted by the strong and sensitive diplomatic hand of Sir Geoffrey Arthur, the last British official to occupy the post of Political Resident in the Gulf.

When the British announced in 1968 that they were withdrawing from lands east of Suez and ending their political control of the Gulf, Dubai's development accelerated.

Since the improvements to the Creek in the 1950s, dhow trade had increased rapidly – especially local, Iranian and Indian dhows – and by the late 1960s, the port was becoming too congested, with an average of 4,000 dhows a year visiting the Creek. Ocean-going vessels had to anchor offshore and were loaded and offloaded by barges.

Anticipating the need for a deep-water harbour at the mouth of the Creek, Sheikh Rashid commissioned a leading international civil engineering consultant in 1965 to undertake a feasibility study. With a loan guaranteed by future oil revenues, work on a small £9 million, four-berth harbour was begun in 1967. The road built to the rock quarry supplying material for the new harbour was the first proper road into the desert.

Even before this first phase was completed, Sheikh Rashid decided to extend the harbour to 15 berths costing some £23 million. Named Mina Rashid, the port opened to sea traffic in 1972, at the time the biggest earthworks project undertaken in Dubai.

Oil production on a limited scale officially began on 6th September 1969, with a tanker carrying the first 180,000 barrels for export on 22nd September 1969. Dubai's second oil field, Southwest Fateh, was discovered in November 1970 coming on stream two years later.

While Abu Dhabi, with huge oil and gas reserves, preferred to build up its reserves, Dubai's approach was to sell aggressively on the open markets. In 1970, Sheikh Rashid pushed the international oil concessionaires for an increase in Dubai's share of the oil revenue to 55 per cent, thereby increasing development revenues as the population grew to over 60,000 – a three-fold increase in 30 years.

The success that followed has been the result of effective collaboration between the two principal Emirates within the UAE. Both Dubai and Abu Dhabi have moved to bridge regional divides, while collaborating across frontiers to enable rapid progress for all their people.

Nurtured in the values of Islam, goodwill and good-neighbourly coexistence and embedded in Bedu traditions of loyalty, chivalry and generosity, stereotypes have been broken and success achieved across a broad range of national and international endeavours.

UNION AND FEDERATION

"Islam is a civilising religion that gives mankind dignity. A Moslem is he who does not inflict evil upon others. Islam is the religion of tolerance and forgiveness, and not of war, but of dialogue and understanding."
(Sheikh Zayed bin Sultan Al Nahayan, President of the UAE and Ruler of Abu Dhabi).

On 1st March 1971, the British Foreign Secretary Sir Alec Douglas-Home made a formal announcement in the House of Commons, declaring that British forces would be withdrawn from the Trucial States by the end of the year.

In July 1971 the seven Rulers met in Dubai as members of the Trucial States Council to discuss the transfer of functions formerly performed by the British Government. On 18th July a communiqué announcing the formation of the United Arab Emirates revealed to the world the Arab world's first and only federal state.

On 2nd December 1971, Britain renounced the maritime agreements of the nineteenth and twentieth century. The 'Temporary Constitution' originally proposed by the British remained in place, simply dropping the word 'temporary'. Under this provisional constitution the Federal Supreme Council, with members from leading merchant families, was established as the highest authority in the country and vested with legislative and executive powers.

Sheikh Zayed bin Sultan Al Nahyan was elected President, and Abu Dhabi was named the federal capital. The position of President is re-elected every five years by the Supreme Council of Rulers.

Sheikh Rashid bin Saeed Al Maktoum was the first Vice-President and later (1979-1990) the Prime Minister of the UAE. The oldest of his four sons Sheikh Maktoum was appointed first Prime Minister and given the task of forming the fledgling state's first cabinet.

In the days after 2nd December, Sheikh Maktoum appointed his brother Sheikh Mohammed bin Rashid Al Maktoum as Minister of Defence. Sheikh Mohammed was the youngest Minister of Defence in the world at the time.

Sheikh Mohammed also became head of the Dubai Central Military Command established in 1971, and his brother Brigadier Sheikh Ahmed bin Rashid became head of the Dubai army.

Pooling sovereignty brought stability and prosperity to the region.

The federal government runs a major part of the country's infrastructure and administrative affairs, while individual Emirates retain their identity with considerable autonomy, thus maintaining healthy competition.

Once the UAE became responsible for its own destiny, development at all levels gained pace. While the help and expertise of many nations was recruited, the federation guided its own progress. Given the resources and the will to change its fortunes, the UAE stands as an example to other states for the effective use of national wealth for the greater good of its peoples.

Inspired by the example of Dubai, Emiratis are becoming increasingly business-minded and industrious, and despite the phenomenal rate of change, the region has not become destabilised. The founding of the United Arab Emirates is marked by a three-day holiday each December, during which parks and public places host cultural activities.

Not long after the formation of the UAE, oil prices quadrupled in 1973 and increased again in 1979, bringing considerable windfalls to these small states with their huge energy resources. Dubai is the second largest oil producer in the UAE after Abu Dhabi, and oil production in the Emirate rose from 250,000 barrels per day in 1970 to 350,000 bpd in 1985, peaking at 410,000 bpd in 1991 before beginning to decline.

During the 1970s, when it became clear to Sheikh Rashid that Dubai could become the most important trading centre in that part of the Gulf, he initiated plans for an international trade centre to provide facilities and accommodation for trade fairs and exhibitions.

Dubai World Trade Centre – the city's first major building project – was completed in 1979. Its 39-storey white tower, then situated on the outskirts of Dubai, was the tallest building in the Middle East and became a landmark symbolising the new Dubai as a beacon for international commerce.

Like many of Sheikh Rashid's ventures, the trade centre was criticised at the time as being a white elephant, yet it has proved an invaluable asset to Dubai. "Sheikh Rashid was a genius. His business acumen had no equal," Sheikh Hasher Mana Al Maktoum has said. "Many people regarded these projects as over ambitious and exercises in futility. But Sheikh Rashid knew that these would be pillars of strength for Dubai, and all his actions were vindicated by later events."

As Dubai became increasingly prosperous, the construction boom transformed the Creek from the area around the souks to Al Maktoum Bridge

PRECEDING PAGE
The 1820 description of Dubai as an "assemblage of mud hovels" bares little resemblance to the striking architecture of this modern Emirate.

with an architectural flair unmatched in any other Middle Eastern state. Such landmark buildings as The National Bank of Dubai, The Emirates Towers, the Chamber of Commerce and Industry, the Etisalat (Communications) Tower and many more examples of eclectic modern architecture sympathetic to local and Islamic designs, capture the visitor's imagination.

In this rush to change, institutions and individuals from all walks of life have been participants, sharing the labour and rewards of enterprise. The thriving banking sector is led by the National Bank of Dubai, the region's most profitable financial institution, established a mere 40 years before. Its Managing Director, Abdullah Saleh, has seen the bank grow from a small office with himself and an assistant as the first employees.

"It is important," he says, "to look at Dubai's incredible transformation with the perspective of one who has lived through the harsh, early years before the advent of change. I can still remember as a child seeing Redha The Tea-maker crossing the Creek on an *abra* with his red-hot charcoal fire ready to serve fresh, hot tea to those attending the Ruler's daily *majlis*.

"We simply didn't have the resources, and even tea-makers were few and far between as coffee is the traditional Bedu drink. There was nothing until the late Sheikh Rashid personally took the reigns of governance in hand. He was a remarkable man, instilling the same energy and drive into his sons who now lead us so ably into the twenty-first century. If I were to conjecture Dubai's future development based on what I have seen over my lifetime, I suspect we will have achieved our common aims of propelling ourselves to the forefront as the commercial, financial and tourist destination of choice between the West and the East. Between New York and London and Hong Kong and Shanghai."

Public amenities were incorporated as an integral part of the burgeoning city. Safa Park, one of the city's main public recreation areas, was established as early as 1975 and includes fairground attractions, barbecue sites and sporting facilities. Visitors can take shade from the heat under lush tropical trees, while flowering shrubs and lawn grass grow on land that was once blazing sand.

More recently, Creekside Park has been developed along a 2.6 kilometre (1.6 mile) stretch of the south side of the Creek between Al Maktoum and Al Garhoud Bridges. Its open-air amphitheatre seats 1,000 and hosts laser and firework shows during the Shopping Festival. In early

2000, the park opened the UAE's first cable car system, which rides 30 metres (98 feet) high, and in 2002 Children's City opened as an entertaining learning zone for young children.

By 1975 Dubai's population had reached 183,000 – another three-fold increase, this time in less than five years. Port Rashid was becoming increasingly busy as a trading and transport hub, and Sheikh Rashid authorised a further extension to a total of 35 berths, completed in 1980. Today, the majority of tonnage through the port is shipped in containers. The port can handle 100 containers or around 1,000 tons an hour. The only bulk cargo it handles is grain for the National Flour Mill, and various refined petroleum products at the oil jetty. Being located close to the town, banks and merchant offices – coupled with the policy of minimising bureaucracy – facilitates an efficient operating system. In 2001, the ship-shaped Dubai Cruise Terminal was added to Port Rashid as the only dedicated passenger complex in the region.

The ambitious Dubai Dry Dock project, launched by Sheikh Rashid to repair and service supertankers travelling between Europe and the Far East, was undertaken by his son Sheikh Mohammed who formed a management company which kick-started the project into the biggest such facility in the Middle East. Today, it operates the shipyard dry-docks that repair over 200 vessels annually from around the world.

In parallel with the Dry Dock project, Sheikh Rashid embarked on a visionary enterprise, envisaging a new city with a major port and a free trade zone (FTZ) at Jebel Ali located 35 kilometres (22 miles) to the south-west of the city. Jebel Ali's deep water and vast amount of space available for development presented scope for a complimentary industrial and distribution port.

Dominating the skyline along the northern shore of the Creek, the polished steel and glass HQ building of the National Bank of Dubai is a stunning architectural creation, recalling the sweeping curves of a dhow's sail.

The Sheikh kept his choice of location secret to maintain the element of surprise. Apparently only two people in the consultancy group assigned the programme knew of his plans. One of them, Mr Neville Allen, relates the story: "I was called at about 4.00am one morning. There was a telephone call saying that Sheikh Rashid was at Jebel Ali and he wanted me there as soon as possible. I went down there and he explained to me that he wanted to build a big harbour. The area where he wanted to construct the port had been used by the Royal Air Force to fire rockets. So we drove around and he told me what size of port he wanted and then asked how much it would cost. I gave him a figure, and then he said, 'Okay, I am going to do it.' My advice to him was that I could not see any good reason for building a harbour of that size because I did not understand the need. But Sheikh Rashid said, 'I know what I am doing.'"

Sheikh Rashid saw Jebel Ali as the cornerstone of Dubai's industrial future, enabling the economy to diversify by broadening its commercial base. The future of Dubai would be based on more than trade and services – manufacturing industries were to make a substantial contribution. Today, over 90 per cent of Dubai's gross domestic product is generated by its non-oil sector.

Construction of Mina (Port) Jebel Ali started in August 1976. The first two quays were ready within 18 months and the port became fully operational in June 1979. The world's largest artificial harbour is one of the few man-made structures visible from space – along with the Great Wall of China and the hugely fantastic new Palm Island residential development complex off Jumeirah beach.

Today, the vast harbour at Jebel Ali provides 67 berths for ocean-going vessels, serving over 150 of the world's major container shipping lines. There are plans to further increase the number of berths to accommodate the steady growth in cargo traffic. The 15 kilometres of quays and two kilometres of wharfs include special zones for petroleum products, containers, dry bulk and forest products.

Sheikh Mohammed designated the area around the port a Free Trade Zone, making it more attractive to potential users. Founded in 1985, Jebel Ali Free Zone (JAFZ) – the first such zone to be established in the region – was initially conceived as the ideal base for multinationals to warehouse and distribute their products in the Gulf. All goods arriving at Jebel Ali that are meant for re-export or transhipment enjoy a 100 per cent custom duty exemption, freedom from way-leave charges and extended free-time storage.

Over the years, the range of industries has grown from distribution to the whole spectrum of manufacturing, trading and services, and their markets have grown to cover the entire world. By the end of 2002, there were around 2,300 companies in the Free Zone from 93 different countries.

The port area also includes the Dubai Aluminium complex (DUBAL) producing 300,000 tons of aluminium a year, the largest in the Middle East, supplying 70 products to 250 customers in 44 countries; the Dubai Gas Plant (DUGAS) which processes all of Dubai's natural gas from the offshore Fateh field; the Cement Works producing half a million tonnes of Portland cement annually; a structural Steelwork Fabrication Workshop; a 300 megawatt steam power station; a desalination plant and an electrical cable plant.

While the Dubai Gas Plant (DUGAS) supplies cheap energy to the large industrial complexes, DUBAL's power generating capability of over 1,400 megawatts is used by the seawater desalination plant to produce 25 million gallons of fresh water every day. The UAE has the second largest per capita water consumption in the world after the USA, using between 100 and 120 gallons a day.

Fresh water production not only serves the needs of a burgeoning consumer-industrial society, but is recycled for reafforestation programmes and desert agri-business complexes that are increasingly supplying the Emirate with a great deal of its vegetable and fresh produce needs.

In May 1981, Sheikh Rashid was struck down by illness and his sons assumed all the responsibilities of running Dubai. They formed an effective leadership trio, with free flow of information and collective decision-making.

Throughout the 1980s, Sheikh Maktoum (then the Crown Prince) had been taking on more duties, paying particular attention to the promotion of law and order and education. He also gained a reputation as a philanthropist, displaying a legendary generosity. He funded a number of humanitarian projects such as handicapped centres, orphanages in developing countries and the construction of schools inside and outside the UAE.

Sheikh Mohammed had taken over the administration of Dubai International Airport (DIA) in 1977, heading a committee to transform passenger and cargo transport to the Emirate. Echoing the earlier approach to Dubai as a leading seaport, he adopted an open-skies policy as a means

Jebel Ali Port, the world's largest man-made harbour, opened in 1979 facilitating the rapid growth of commercial activity, including repair of shipping and construction of off-shore oil and gas platforms.

to fast-track development for Dubai to become the region's aviation and tourist hub.

Since the formation of the UAE, air traffic to Dubai has shown exponential growth. A £6.8 million terminal with a three-storey, air-conditioned building capable of handling 1,200 passengers with a 3,800-metre (12,500-foot) runway able to take Jumbo jets and Concordes, was opened by Sheikh Rashid as early as May 1971.

In December 1983 Dubai Duty Free was established at Dubai International Airport and recorded a first year turnover of US$20 million. By the time the new shopping complex in the futuristic new airport complex at Sheikh Rashid Terminal was opened in 2000, turnover had grown eleven-fold to US$220 million. With its vast shopping emporia selling everything from gold, jewellery, perfumes and electronics to local exotica, Dubai Duty Free had sales exceeding US$280 million last year.

With the population of Dubai increasing from 276,000 in 1980 to 419,000 by 1985 and numbers of transit visitors on the increase, Sheikh Mohammed, embodiment of the new driving force for change in Dubai, decided to create a new international airline from scratch.

A small team was chosen to develop the concept in secret and in October of that year, Emirates Airlines flew for the first time. Within 17 years it has grown to become one of the world's six most profitable and one of the 20 largest international fleet carriers.

Sheikh Ahmed bin Saeed Al Maktoum, President of the Department of Civil Aviation and Chairman of Emirates Airlines, states, "It is Dubai's lifestyle, open-skies aviation policy, weather, geographic location and its hard working people, both nationals and expatriates, that have contributed to Dubai's economic wealth. The airport and Emirates are just part of that team and infrastructure."

An airport extension programme including a new arrivals terminal was completed in 1986, making Dubai the major gateway to the Gulf, serving more than 10,000 passengers a day at the time. The airport's futuristic air traffic control tower and aircraft-shaped Emirates training college demonstrate the Emirate's flamboyant eye for architecture that was beginning to transform the Dubai skyline.

The US$550 million Sheikh Rashid Terminal was opened in April 2000 and, within two years, the airport was handling over 15 million passengers a year, with 100 airlines operating over 10,000 scheduled flights a month and over 2,000 non-scheduled and military flights a month to 137 destinations.

Meanwhile, the Dubai Airport Free Zone (DAFZ) opened alongside the airport in 1999 and established facilities for a wide variety of technology-driven industries and commercial distribution services to further broaden Dubai's base from being a distribution hub to a manufacturing centre that complements the Jebel Ali Free Zone. Today, its 200 high technology and luxury goods companies include Dell, Rolex, Rolls Royce, Porsche and Chanel.

During the Dubai 2001 Airshow, at a time when most airlines were recoiling in the aftermath of September 11 attacks in New York, Emirates Airline ordered US$15 billion worth of new aircraft from Airbus and Boeing, including the double-decker Airbus and the 444-seater Boeing 777-300. Emirates Airlines plans to expand its fleet from 47 to 100 aircraft by 2010, servicing some 50 million passengers annually.

The current US$2.5 billion expansion of DIA incorporates a second runway, runway extensions, new aprons, taxiways, roads, underground tunnels and new warehousing for Dubai Duty Free. Together with Terminal 3 and two concourses for the exclusive use of Emirates Airline, and a Mega

Dubai Duty Free was a success from the moment it was established at Dubai International Airport in 1983, and has now reached a turnover of US$300 million a year, from its first year turnover of US$20 million.

Cargo Terminal at Dubai Cargo Village, the airport expects to be able to handle any passenger increases in traffic well into the foreseeable future.

Meanwhile, the growth of Dubai was benefiting from major investment in its education system. By the 1980s, many local students had begun to graduate in fields previously the preserve of expatriate professionals. Now, local architects were introducing creative styles reflecting traditional Arab designs as well as incorporating influences of Asian and European ideas. The National Bank of Dubai's headquarters building, completed in the late 1990s, is one of the many edifices that architecturally recreate the sail motifs reflected in many of Dubai's landmark structures.

The Creek Golf and Yacht Club took its inspiration from the triangular sails of the lateen-rigged Arab dhows in a diminutive echo of the Sydney Opera House. In 1999, the PGA Dubai Desert Classic golf tournament moved to the Creek Golf and Yacht Club from the Emirates Golf Club – the Gulf's first championship lawn golf course – which had opened in 1988.

From the Creek, developers shifted their attention to the empty land leading from the World Trade Centre away from the city along the Sheikh Zayed Road towards Abu Dhabi. A corridor of high-rise steel and glass structures now strides out along the exit routes from town, pronouncing Dubai's newly-charged confidence as if announcing: We're successful, and proud of it.

Following a long illness, Sheikh Rashid died on 7th October 1990. His eldest son, Sheikh Maktoum became Vice-President and Prime Minister of the UAE, and Ruler of Dubai. Yet it was his brother, Sheikh Mohammed, who has most noticeably inherited his father's vision, hard-working drive and progressive ideas.

When the 40-day Gulf War ended on 4th March 1991, Sheikh Mohammed issued a statement marking the Emirate's first involvement in an active war zone: "The United Arab Emirates will continue to stand for peace… steadfast in her support for her friends. The Emirates remain a cosmopolitan meeting place, where differing cultures and religions reside in peace. It is this model of tolerance that we hope to export to the rest of the world…"

In the 1990s, Sheikh Mohammed was given responsibility for Dubai's oil sector. The Dubai Strategic Plan, drawn up in 1996, indicated that Dubai's oil reserves would run out by 2010. Recognising the risks of relying too heavily on a single source of income, the Rulers encouraged further diversification by dramatically rebuilding and improving the Emirate's infrastructure, adding alternative industries and creating more favourable operating conditions for international and local companies.

In January 1995 Sheikh Mohammed was appointed Defence Minister of the UAE and Crown Prince of Dubai, while his elder brother Sheikh Hamdan became UAE Minister of Finance and Deputy Ruler of the Emirate.

Under the tourism banner 'Destination Dubai,' Sheikh Mohammed announced in late 1995 the creation of the Dubai Shopping Festival, an annual event falling in March/April intended to bring together all aspects of the Emirate's economy as part of a worldwide promotion. The first Shopping Festival succeeded in attracting 1.6 million visitors.

In a carnival atmosphere, the festival incorporates a variety of tourist activities with entertainment events and funfairs, as well as citywide discounts at participating retail outlets with lower prices fixed by the Government. The success of the Shopping Festival led to a second major festival – Dubai Summer Surprises – each year between June and September. The Emirate's most unlikely leisure complex opened during Dubai Summer Surprises 2003, Snow World provides a 600-metre-long ski slope adjacent to Emirates Lakes in the middle of what was until recently scrubland and desert.

As the centrepiece of the Dubai Shopping Festival, Sheikh Mohammed instigated the Dubai World Cup, the world's richest horse race with a purse of US$15 million. Since its inauguration the World Cup, which is held at Nad Al Sheba racecourse in the last week of March, has become a major international event in its own right and a highlight of the global equestrian calendar, attracting crowds of 35,000 at a time.

Although no gambling is permitted in Islam, big prize money guarantees television sports coverage around the world. The 2,000-metre (10-furlong) title race attracts the world's finest and most expensive thoroughbreds from the USA, UK, France, Australia and Japan.

Visitors to the Nad Al Sheba Club can view the state-of-the-art training facilities and the Godolphin Gallery, where the world-beating exploits of the Dubai-based stables are commemorated, including the Dubai World Cup trophy itself, first won by the American racehorse *Great Cigar* in 1996, ridden by jockey Jerry Bailey.

The ruling family first began to formalise horse racing in Dubai when Sheikh Maktoum bin Rashid Al Maktoum constructed the Sheikhdom's

first racetrack in Deira in 1969. This is now home to the Dubai Equine Hospital, one of the most advanced in the world. During the 1970s, the Al Ghussais track hosted the UAE's first regular race meetings, while Sheikh Mohammed built up his stables at Zabeel.

When land was needed for the new international airport in 1984, Al Ghussais closed and attention turned to Nad Al Sheba on even ground t the end of the Creek. Under trainer Bill Mather, Nad Al Sheba Stables quickly became the most competitive in the Emirates.

Sheikh Hamdan bin Rashid Al Maktoum oversaw the development of the specialist Zabeel Feed Mill, while Sheikh Ahmed bin Rashid Al Maktoum had a hand in the unique Jebel Ali track with its innovative oil-and-sand mix racing surface.

Like his brothers, Sheikh Maktoum and Sheikh Hamdan, Sheikh Mohammed is a keen horse breeder, with mainly French and American bloodlines. Besides his farm at Hatta, Sheikh Mohammed has stud farms in France, England and the United States. He is the largest breeder of *asil* (pure-bred) Arab racehorses and one of the world's largest breeders of thoroughbreds with over 3,000 horses in training around the world, winning major international events in France, UK and USA. In 1995 the now-legendary thoroughbred Lammtarra, bred from his own stables, achieved the historic treble of the Derby at Epsom, the King George VI and Queen Elizabeth Stakes at Ascot, and Paris's Prix de l'Arc de Triomphe, a feat only managed once before by Mill Reef in 1971.

Sheikh Mohammed has moved most of his breeding and training activities to Dubai, naming his stud Godolphin after one of the three founding stallions of the modern thoroughbred. At the beginning of the eighteenth century, many Arabian horses were bought by British noblemen to improve their bloodstocks. Three of them – the Byerley Turk, Godolphin Barb and Darley Arabian – are progenitors of all the thoroughbred horses now in existence.

Once again, Sheikh Mohammed confounded critics who muttered at the time that the desert conditions were not conducive to world-class horse breeding. As the world's largest breeder of fine horses, the Sheikh proved them wrong by training trophy winners right under the desert sun.

Recounting stories from his first horse buying trip to Newmarket in England some quarter of a century ago, Sheikh Mohammed remembers the lukewarm reception he received from sellers and auctioneers: "They didn't take me seriously, and I determined there and then that I would have the best and largest breeding stables in the world before the turn of the century." Like most things he set his mind to, the Sheikh succeeded with a few years to spare.

Sheikh Mohammed's keen personal interest in the revival of the Arab *asil* breed has led to his own hands-on breeding of Arabs in his various Dubai horse farms and European and American studs. An avid sportsman, huntsman, falconer and championship rider, Sheikh Mohammed has re-established desert endurance racing in the region and is himself often found riding in 100-kilometre races lasting 24 hours or more across inhospitable desert terrain under searing heat and dust. Always leading from the front, the Sheikh has single-handedly transformed the landscape of global thoroughbred and Arab horse racing.

Arab horses also make excellent polo ponies and the Dubai Polo Club holds matches throughout the winter. Moray Brown, a renowned polo player of the early twentieth century, admired the qualities of the Arab horse: "They have brains, and in fact they take to the game and understand it sooner than an English pony will."

Major international sporting events have helped establish Dubai as the sports capital of the Middle East, ensuring a prominent place for the Emirate on the world sporting events calendar. Besides golf and horse racing, Dubai hosts the annual US$1.5 million Dubai Tennis Championships organised by Dubai Duty Free, held in the second week of February.

The Dubai-based Victory team is a frequent winner of the cup in the UIM Class One World Offshore powerboat championships in October or November in the waters off Le Méridien Al Mina Al Siyahi.

The UAE Desert Challenge puts cars and motorcycles through a tough course across the desert between Dubai and Abu Dhabi, while the Autodrome and Business Park which opened in 2003, provides world-class motor racing facilities, including a five-kilometre asphalt track built to Formula One specifications.

The two-day Dubai Rugby Sevens tournament is held during the three-day public holiday to commemorate the foundation of the UAE, and the biennial Dubai Airshow is a trade event attracting global attention from aerial and flying enthusiasts.

Besides swimming, tennis and badminton, participation sports include shooting and archery at Hatta Fort Hotel and Jebel Ali Hotel. Dune-bashing is the local term for the adventurous (and highly dangerous) activity involving four-wheel-drive vehicles or quad bikes racing across hilly sand dunes over treacherous off-road terrain. Many tourists enjoy the adventure by being driven by professional outfits such as Arabian Adventures. Not something to be recommended for the faint-hearted, but an experience well worth the adrenalin waste.

While sporting events have generated a healthy local following,

they have also helped energise in-bound tourism. The warm climate with its year-round guarantee of sunshine provides the basic ingredient for beach holidays, while the desert heritage offers the backdrop to four-wheel-drive and camel safaris, culminating in dune banquets under the stars.

Add to this the culture and character of old Dubai, and the ever-increasing number of sophisticated amenities, and the international traveller will stay longer than it takes just to stock up on duty free goods. World-class hotels, golf courses that are turning the desert green, theme parks to rival those in America or Japan and a vast new marina go to make the mix that is increasingly attracting European sun-seekers to Dubai in ever larger numbers.

The Miami-style US$4.35 billion Dubai Marina, scooped out of the Jumeirah desert, is billed as a city within a city. Intended to accommodate over 150,000 people in a mix of low, medium and high-rise buildings, the project is scheduled for completion in 2008.

Under the Chairmanship of Sheikh Mohammed, the Department of Tourism & Commercial Marketing (DTCM) was established in 1997 to promote Dubai internationally, and today tourism is booming, rivalling some

of the world's most popular established destinations. The number of visitors increased from 1.8m in 1997 to over 3m in 2000. And following the savvy international advertising campaigns funded by the Department of Civil Aviation and Dubai Duty Free in 2002, the Emirate expects visitor figures to reach 15 million by 2010.

International hotel chains have rushed to join Dubai's success story – Sheraton, Hilton, Hyatt, Fairmont, Taj, Shangri-La, Ritz-Carlton, Le Méridien, Kerzner International and many others. All cater for the expanding conference market as well as leisure tourism, with extensive meeting facilities and incentive programmes.

Martin Brodie, head of corporate media relations for Rolls Royce, which chose Dubai for its first public relations conference outside the UK bringing together delegates from 14 different countries, observes: "Dubai offers some of the best conference facilities in the world and real value for money."

As the focus for the IMF World Bank meeting in September 2003, the first of its kind to be held in the Middle East, the purpose-built convention centre attached to the World Trade Centre is, appropriately, the largest in the Middle East capable of seating up to 6,000 delegates in a multi-purpose hall.

Former Director General of the Dubai Technology, E-Commerce and Media Free Zone and Chairman of the Dubai Internet City, Mohammed Al Gergawi, emphasises the city's growing importance as a conference destination when he writes: "Dubai and the UAE has had a regional reputation for being primarily an exhibitions centre. In recent times, it has increasingly become known as a regional conference centre. But now, with the success of major international meetings, the country's reputation has been extended worldwide."

As tourism has flourished, so has the Jumeirah Beach area. Jumeirah and neighbouring Umm Suqeim were already among the city's wealthiest residential areas, with west-facing beaches, modern restaurants, small shopping malls, sailing clubs, a zoo, waterfront parks and hotels. The beaches are clean, safe and seldom crowded, and the sun shines virtually every day of the year. At night, the luminescent microscopic sea creatures give off a blue-green light when disturbed by swimmers on the beach.

It is a setting ready-made for tourism and the Jumeirah International Hotel Group has developed a number of headline-catching concepts along this coastline. The 618-room, 26-storey Jumeirah Beach Hotel shaped like a breaking wave, made quite a splash when it opened in 1997, only to be overshadowed in December 1999 by its even more flamboyant neighbour, the Burj Al Arab (Arabian Tower) soaring 321 metres above a man-made island some 100 metres offshore.

The all-suite Burj Al Arab is so impressive and distinctive a structure that it immediately became the city's most recognisable icon. Taller than the Eiffel Tower and just 60 metres shorter than the Empire State Building, it is the tallest hotel in the world. Its billowing sail shape is dazzling white by day and becomes the screen for colourful light displays at night.

Attached to the Jumeirah Beach Hotel, the Wild Wadi theme park opened in 1999. Every day two million gallons of water are pumped through tunnels, tubes, slides, caves and pools to the delight of young and old escaping heat and sun.

On the mainland next to the Burj Al Arab, the new 940-room Arabian oasis of hotels and villas – Madinat Jumeirah – evokes the atmosphere of old Dubai, with *abras* plying three kilometres of waterways passing souks and wind-towers, while guests are cushioned in modern luxury.

Along the coast, adjacent to the Dubai Marina, is the Palace of the Royal Mirage, a hotel fit for royalty that provides Arabian hospitality within the sumptuous surroundings of a traditional Arabian palace. The Royal Mirage has expanded into three adjoining properties, each with its own identity and privacy, considered by many to be one of the finest hotels in Dubai.

Further along the coast is the Sheraton Jumeirah Beach Resort. "Jumeirah must be one of the most dynamic areas on the planet – expansion is non-stop and the place is being transformed, virtually in front of your eyes," enthuses general manager Jorg Heyer. "While unspoilt beaches and the warm blue waters of the Gulf would alone be irresistible tourist magnets, the sheer scale and pace of complementary development is catapulting Jumeirah from a well-kept secret to the place to see and be seen."

In the heart of the desert, the luxurious and exclusive Al Maha Desert Resort, the Emirates Group cameo hotel, is the first eco-tourism resort in the region working to reintroduce the Arabian oryx, sand gazelle, mountain gazelle, Arabian fox and caracal back into Dubai. "Tourism is the only industry that can fund conservation," says its general manager.

An area of 225 square kilometres is being fenced off to protect vegetation from overgrazing by camels and goats, and to preserve the pristine desert landscape from the encroachments of urban degradation.

Considering that this is five per cent of Dubai's territorial landmass, the project is as ambitious as it is environmentally courageous. Spearheaded by Sheikh Ahmed bin Saeed Al Maktoum, this project is emblematic of the dynamism that drives the Emirate to act decisively for the general interest of the people and future well-being of their ecosystem.

In March 2000, Sheikh Mohammed told London's Sunday Telegraph newspaper: "I have a vision. I look to the future, 20, 30 years. I learnt that from my father, Sheikh Rashid. He is the true father of modern Dubai. I follow his example. He would rise early and go alone to watch what was happening on each of his projects. I do the same. I watch. I read faces. I take decisions and I move fast. Full throttle."

That same month, Sheikh Mohammed launched the Information Technology Education Project for secondary schools, emphasising the priority given to education in twenty-first-century Dubai. The project ensures that the youth of Dubai are familiar with the latest technology when they leave school, and that qualified nationals will be ready to take up employment in the IT industry.

Dubai has long provided a comprehensive education system for boys and girls, with free education for nationals in government schools, colleges and universities. In 1975, the rate of adult literacy was 54.2 per cent amongst men, and 30.9 per cent amongst women. By 1998, it was 73.4 per cent amongst men and 77.1 per cent amongst the women.

The percentage of women workers more than trebled between 1980 and 1990, rising from 5.3 per cent to 16.3 per cent of the total workforce. And the majority of students at UAE University and the Higher Colleges of Technology (HCT) are now women. Zayed University for women opened in 1998, and by 1999, female students regularly performed better than their male counterparts.

Perhaps the boldest new front in Dubai's plans has been 'e-Dubai'. On October 29, 1999 Sheikh Mohammed called a press conference where he announced: "One year from today, we will inaugurate, on this site, a new initiative, not only for Dubai but for the rest of the world. We call it Dubai Internet City."

His vision involved an Internet City that would encompass the

infrastructure, environment and attitude to enable new economy enterprises to operate out of Dubai with significant competitive advantages.

Despite early scepticism, Dubai Internet City (DIC) was launched in October 2000 and soon had to expand in response to demand. This initiative was followed in January 2001 by Dubai Media City (DMC), which together with Dubai Knowledge Village make up the Dubai Technology, E- Commerce and Media Free Zone – a central feature of Dubai's future plans.

Phase One of Media City was sold-out within 18 months of its opening. By 2002, DIC and DMC were home to over 450 companies, including such international giants as Microsoft, Hewlett-Packard, IBM, Reuters, CNN and Middle East Broadcasting Corporation (MBC).

This free zone is also helping to introduce the next generation of leaders in the Al Maktoum family to their responsibilities – the Chairman is Sheikh Maktoum bin Mohammed Al Maktoum, Sheikh Mohammed's third son.

Another piece in the jigsaw of the Al Maktoum family's plans for the future is the e-government project. The Dubai e-government portal opened in October 2001, giving Dubai the world's first fully online government services. The people of Dubai can now use the Internet to renew and apply for all kinds of licences, pay fines, request information and much more. For anyone familiar with stifling bureaucracies in the region, this form of conducting government business with minimal cost, time and effort is a dream which has come true before its time, and even before the most advanced countries of the world.

Dubai has also moved into the world of international finance, with the opening in February 2002 of the Dubai International Financial Centre (DIFC) that Sheikh Mohammed announced would "be a bridge for financial services between our region and the international markets 24 hours a day and seven days a week ... This centre will provide an ideal business environment based on a highly developed infrastructure and control regulations and laws that rival the latest and most competent regulations and laws worldwide."

This highly ambitious US$5 billion project envisages a fully independent, stand-alone financial centre in league with such global poles of money and expertise as Hong Kong and Singapore, with regulatory standards on a par with London and New York. The first phase of DIFC will be completed by 2004, making Dubai the only competitor in the Middle East and the Gulf region to such powerhouses as Frankfurt and Sydney, London and Hong Kong as a one-stop financial centre.

Early in 2001, Sheikh Mohammed announced by far the most extraordinary 'Destination Dubai' project to date. The Palms, a US$3 billion resort project that will add a total of 120 kilometres of waterfront to Dubai's 72-kilometre coastline, is stunning in its ambitious reach.

This resort will be spread over two man-made, palm tree-shaped islands, each of which is made up of an archipelago in the shape of 17 huge fronds and the trunk, surrounded by a crescent-shaped island, the back of which forms a protective breakwater. The islands measure five kilometres by five kilometres and the crescent island extends for 11 kilometres, making them the largest man-made islands in the world. The crescent will hold up to 40 hotels, including the Kempinski, Hilton and Le Méridien, while the 'fronds' will house 2,000 residential units and the 'trunk' will have nine hotels, two marinas, a variety of retail and recreational facilities.

"The world has not yet seen anything like Palm Island," says Ali Saeed Albwardi, Chairman of the Albwardi Investment Group. "It is ambitious, inspiring and truly unique in keeping with, but going even further than the exceptional developments already undertaken by private investors and the Dubai Government during recent years."

LEFT
Crown Prince Sheikh Mohammed (to the right) with Sheikh Ahmed bin Saeed Al Maktoum, President of Dubai Civil Aviation and Chairman of Emirates Airlines, engrossed in deep conversation.

RIGHT
Dubai Media City provides the infrastructure and business environment to enable media-related enterprises, for example, CNN, Reuters and MBC, to operate globally without restrictions out of Dubai. This venture is unique in the entire Arab world.

ABOVE
Dubai International Financial Centre is a US$5 billion project intended to make Dubai the fully independent, one-stop finanacial hub of the Middle East, on a par with Hong Kong and Singapore. The first phase, appropriately named The Gateway (above) is due for completion in 2004, while the whole project will be up and running by 2005.

The first of the two islands is located off Jumeirah beach and the second will be constructed south-west of Jebel Ali Port, scheduled for completion in 2006. While The Palm Jumeirah will focus on residential and leisure, The Palm Jebel Ali will be developed as an activity and entertainment complex on a 'Sea Village' concept.

Meanwhile, back at the Creek, the US$1.65 billion Dubai Festival City will, by 2006, introduce a four-kilometre waterfront development in Al Garhoud, combining a 8,000-seat open-air amphitheatre, entertainment, dining, shopping, a marina, hotels, offices and residential apartments.

"Our unwavering aim is to make this the best place to do business, the top tourist destination and transport hub in the region, and to be the undisputed commercial and communications capital of the Middle East," Sheikh Mohammed forcefully explains.

Vision, ingenuity and determination have enabled the people of the Emirate to make full use of existing and timely opportunities. Early inhabitants used its strategic location on a vital trading route to develop commerce. Trade that began 7,000 years ago with earthen pots from Mesopotamia expanded to include frankincense, pearls, gold, herbs and spices. Textiles, grain and wood have in more recent times been replaced by high technology and electronic goods; in fact, every kind of commodity that goes to service its own fledgling modern economy, and for re-export beyond its shores.

In steering Dubai towards the realisation of its Rulers' dream as a cornerstone of peace and prosperity in the region, the Al Maktoum family have uncorked the energies of its own populace and garnered the talents of peoples drawn from the four corners of the globe.

Given free reign to exploit latent opportunities, locals have taken to the task of building their city-state with energy unmatched anywhere else in the Arabian Peninsula.

Always mindful of their origins, true to traditions and the positive tenets of Islam, the Dubai people have turned stereotypes on their heads, showing the world that Arabian dreams can match the aspirations of hard-working people.

Dubai is an experiment in the making, a work in progress. An example of how the effective mix of tradition, religion and enterprise woven into a modern fabric can transform the most steadfast and tradition-based of societies without compromising those finer qualities that the desert has bequeathed through centuries.

By the time oil arrived, Dubai was already an important regional trading centre, despite the trauma and decline brought on by the collapse of the pearling industry early in the last century. Oil wealth was not vast, but sufficient to catalyse Ruler and ruled into a scramble for development against the draining resource clock of indigent energy supplies.

Inevitably, the process of rapid change erodes traditional values. Yet Dubai has kept itself rooted in its heritage, ever mindful of the dangers of disassociation, which helter-skelter progress can engender.

The trappings of prosperity have not blurred the vision of its Rulers, and the Al Maktoums have consciously sought to retain and reinvigorate facets of their cultural and environmental heritage.

The Dubai Wildlife and Waterbird Sanctuary at the southern tip of the Creek, the Dubai Museum, Sheikh Saeed's House and Heritage Village are among the many reminders of the richness of the past that have been preserved and reconstructed to inform the present and guide the future.

Many residents can today still recall playing *Luhol* and *Huwaim* –

Of the many projects spearheaded by Crown Prince Sheikh Mohammed, the Palm Island is perhaps the most spectacular. Two vast archipelagos in the shape of palm trees are being created offshore at Jumeirah and Jebel Ali, adding 120 kilometres to Dubai's 72-kilometre coastline. The US$3 billion resort complex will feature hotels, residential, recreational and shopping facilities. From concept to execution to realisation, these three images show the progress of this huge project.

tag and hopscotch – as children by the *Arish* houses clustered around the Creek. They remember hauling water from wells in goat-skin buckets, walking past cud-chewing camels couched outside courtyards. They can still hear the hissing kerosene lamps that cast shadows, as the night watchman did his rounds winding his way through the narrow alleyways of Bastakia.

The image of desert warriors of yore, bravery and chivalry in the face of unrelenting hardships shared by all, still spur older Dubai folk to poetic reflection. Sitting in the splendours of modern comforts unimaginable even thirty years before, all agree that good fortune has smiled upon them and the *baraka* of Allah has helped them through troubling and testing times.

People remember watching the almost bewildering transformation of their unique city-state in their short lifetimes. Electricity, running water, luxury cars and five-lane highways stretching their tentacles out into the desert sands where once only camels roamed in search of grazing. Gleaming towers of steel and glass, giant buildings each reflecting the moods of the rising and setting sun – monuments to the transforming power of modern man in league with breathless technology.

Dubai is growing so fast that you have to keep redrawing your mental map of the Emirate every time you visit. New shopping malls, office complexes and residential areas are carved from desert, mountains and from the sea; rocks forming the foundations of new lands born on the Gulf's shores.

Sleek luxury cars and four-wheel-drive vehicles glide like shimmering mirages in the mid-day desert heat, heading towards hotels, golf courses and marinas that did not exist five years before.

The destiny of the Emirate of Dubai is driven by a vision that understands the need for diversification in ensuring a stable future. "While reaching for our goals, we must break away from what's routine, and make creativity intrinsic to everything we do," is how Sheikh Mohammed describes his own visionary goal.

While the late Sheikh Rashid is often proclaimed the father of modern Dubai, it is his children who today help to propel Dubai into realms beyond the wildest dreams of their ancestors, beyond the imaginings borne out of tales from the Arabian Nights.

A respect for tradition enriches the present with values developed through centuries of hardship. Qualities of determination, loyalty, honour and generosity helped the people to survive in the past and those same attributes help to underwrite a dazzling future for Dubai.

"The more effort you put in, the more you achieve. Glory requires many sleepless nights."
(Ninth-century Arab saying)

THE LAND

ABOVE
Calligonum comosum, *locally called* arta, *provides the desert firewood. Young shoots are eaten as salad greens and the bright-red seedpods provide a spicy condiment, while the whole plant stabilises the loose sand and acts as a windbreak.*

LEFT
The Graceful warbler is one of the smallest birds of Dubai – about 10 centimetres long. A year-round resident, it is easier heard than seen as its loud cries proclaim its territory throughout the year. The nest is skilfully constructed, with a downy soft inside and small round opening, sometimes shaded by a small cantilevered awning.

ABOVE
The saltbush Halopeplis perfoliata stores salty water in its bead-like leaves and provides food for hares and livestock even in times of drought.

LEFT

Compacted sand eroded by the wind in the vicinity of Lahbab. These strange formations can reach considerable heights, with the wind erosion creating mushroom-like structures underneath which gazelles shelter during the mid-day heat.

BELOW

The wonders of nature displayed in the fierce heat of unforgiving climes, as seasonal rains bring the desert to life with wild flowers of every colour, shape and form, like these Eremobium aegyptiacum spreading their shadows like spiders across the sand. Eremobium *derives its name form the Greek words* ermos *meaning desert and* bios *meaning life. Spring ephemerals, these flowers germinate, flower and seed within a few weeks of the spring rains.*

74

The Dubai Wildlife and Waterbird Sanctuary at Ras Al Khor at the inland end of the Creek attracts a wintering colony of up to 1,500 Greater flamingos (Phoenicopterus ruber)*, many of which have opted to stay year-round. In 1985 an artificial island was built and the protected birds are supplied with supplementary food at man-made feeding stations.*

Dubai's many parks and landscaped roadside gardens display a great variety of cultivated plants. The brilliant red hibiscus blooms all year adding vibrant flashes of colour.

Backlit by the early morning sunlight, a hoopoe searches the grass for insects.

The terrain supports a rich, though elusive, diversity of wildlife, now largely protected and nurtured through environmental programmes. The spiny-tailed agama (Uromastyx aegypticus) *is so well adapted to harsh desert conditions that it has not needed to change its appearance or lifestyle in 25,000 years.*

The cream and yellow frangipani *(Plumeria acuminato) has a sweet aromatic scent and can be founding many parks and gardens, whilst the Sodom's Apple,* or Calotropis procera *(below) adds colour and fruit in temperatures that can reach 55 Centigrade in the shade at the height of summer.*

LEFT
*These extraordinary
'sand waterfalls'
are one of Dubai's
intriguing natural
phenomena. These
sandfalls occur when
the sand is removed
from behind dunes,
creating a vacuum
with the onrush of
the sand roaring
over the edges.*

RIGHT
*The striated rocks
near Hatta show their
colours best in the
late afternoon sun.*

LEFT
During the autumn migration 27,000 birds have been recorded at one time at the Dubai Wildlife and Waterbird Santuary.

ABOVE
The grey heron is a winter visitor to Dubai.

ABOVE
Marine fossils in the limestone mountains at the edge of the gravel plains point to the fact that these were once beaches of the Tethys Sea-some 75 million years ago. More than thirty species of fossilised sea-urchins have been identified, some of which are now extinct. Gastropods like these are very common all over limestone mountains in Dubai.

RIGHT
The stark lines of the Hajar Mountains in the east of Dubai receive sporadic winter rainfall that transforms dry wadis (river beds) into raging torrents. These flash floods disappear quickly, replenishing the underground water-table. These floods can be very dangerous, as more people are killed by them every year than by the desert heat.

85

LEFT

A popular spot for picnickers and a place to cool off, Hatta Pools are one of the few examples in the region of natural surface water.

RIGHT

Air escaping from the mud in a sand pool after rains sometimes creates the appearance of a bed of pearls bubbling from the desert.

CULTURE AND TRADITION

88

Glazed pottery vases, jars and pots have been unearthed at different archaeological sites in Dubai. Excavations at Jumeirah, one of the main ancient trade routes between Mesopotamia (Iraq) and Oman passing through this region, reveal ninth and tenth-century influences from Iraq and Syria.

The walls of Sheikh Saeed Al Maktoum's House in Shindagha were built in 1896 using coral quarried from the Gulf and the Creek, then covered with lime and plaster. Home to the Ruling Family until 1958, the house has now been restored and is open to the public.

LEFT
Much of Sheikh Saeed's House has been preserved or renovated to demonstrate the Dubai way of life in pre-oil days. Above the well in the extensive courtyard hangs an original goat-skin bucket.

ABOVE LEFT, RIGHT
*Walls, roofs and
fences were
constructed using
readily available
fronds of the
palm tree.*

Wind-towers have been restored or reconstructed in Heritage Village in the Shindagha district as part of an active policy to preserve traditional aspects of Dubai lifestyles.

LEFT
A century ago, before the advent of air-conditioning, architectural designs focused on the need to utilise the cooling breezes through wind-towers, while minimising the fierce effect of the sun's heat.

ABOVE
Watch-towers like this one in Hatta, were positioned on high ground close to wells and irrigated land to give advanced warning of hostile raiders, and afford refuge for farmers and herdsmen.

LEFT
*Vernacular
architecture was
designed to keep out
the summer heat.
Narrow, shaded
streets and alleyways
and small, paneless
windows positioned
high above the road
level, excluded
the sunlight while
encouraging cooling
breezes.*

RIGHT
A dhow *passes the
Bastakia district
alongside Dubai
Creek.*

Encouraged and supported by the Ruling Family, skilled craftsmen still use traditional methods, techniques and materials in the building of dhows, working with their hands and shaping the wood by eye only.

LEFT
*This example of
ancient gypsum
carvings dating back
a millennia, excavated
in archaeological
digs in Jumeirah,
shows a remarkable
similarity to the
wood carvings found
today above the
entrance doors to the
old houses of Dubai.*

ABOVE AND RIGHT
*Decoratively carved
teak doors borrowed
designs from
Indian and
regional influences,
traditionally
incorporating stellar
or floral motifs.
Complete doors were
often carved in India
and shipped to Dubai.*

LEFT
Camels can drink up to 12 gallons of water at a time, then survive without it for up to six months in winter, as long as they can feed on sparse desert vegetation.

ABOVE
Goats are the mainstay of the Bedouin livestock, supplying milk and meat, while their skins were used to make tents, buckets and clothing.

RIGHT
For thousands of years, irrigation systems (aflaj) have channelled water to palm groves and other areas of cultivation. Some of these old irrigation channels are being actively restored.

The date palm (Phoenix dactylifera) earned its title 'prince of trees' by providing one of the few sources of high-calorie foods, as well as versatile building materials used in the construction of houses and small boats, such as the inshore shashah made of palm fronds. The fruit is cut just before it is ripe, and can be kept indefinitely when dried. There are 36 varieties of dates in the Emirates alone, grown in small palm groves and large plantations.

Inhabitants of this coastline are now less dependent on harvests from the sea as a main source of protein, but the morning fish market in Dubai is still awash with a great variety of species, including red snapper, belt fish, kingfish, sardines and baby sharks, washed and filleted by workers in blue uniforms. Sun-dried, the sardine-like doma are used as fodder for livestock, or as fertiliser.

LEFT
Sardine nets are left overnight and the fishermen pull them in at dawn, trapping the fish which are then collected with buckets and dried onshore. Smoked or salted, the sardines are mixed with desert herbs and spices and eaten as a side-dish to enhance the flavour of local cuisine.

BELOW
Baby sharks are a particular delicacy in the region. Cut into thin, small pieces, marinated and mixed with spices, the 'Jeshid' is eaten with dried, black lemons. Local folklore has it that it is a potent aphrodisiac.

Falcons were traditionally caught and trained at the time of the migration of the houbara bustard – the preferred fighting prey. Today, the bustard is protected but falconry remains the most sought after social pastime amongst young and old alike, with its strong echoes of the desert Arab's heritage.

ABOVE LEFT
A falconer tenderly feeds his bird after a desert hunt (middle) Villager living in a typical stone mountain house

FARE RIGHT
While old friends greet each other with joy.

LEFT

Arabic coffee (qahwah) is the national refreshment of the social Emirati, drunk in small cups without handles. After repeated servings, the cup is rocked back and forth to indicate that no more is required. Long hours are spent around fires conversing, reciting poetry and recounting the deeds of myth and legend, as well as arguing over the price of goods and shipments of produce.

RIGHT

Many men carry prayer beads (mespah) with them at all times in recognition of the ever-present influence of Islam in their lives. There is a whole culture surrounding the types and makes of prayer beads, with some rare jewels making them valuable beyond the reach of all but the rich.

LEFT

Poured from a hornbill-spouted coffee-pot (dalla) of brass or copper, cardamom flavoured black coffee is the traditional drink of the desert Beduoin. The dalla itself is, with the falcon, the national symbol of the UAE.

RIGHT

The burning of agar wood from Malaysia produces a rich, sweet fragrance, which has been enjoyed after dinner since the time of Sinbad.

ABOVE
The ayala *is a typical dance in the Emirates, where men use their walking sticks (asaaa) to the rhythmic chant of the drums.*

Traditional song and dance draw inspiration from life in the desert, the mountains and from the sea, assimilating influences from many other cultures. Such displays can now only be seen at special events and *national celebrations. Men and women gather separately to chant and sway to the rhythm of animal-skin drums. But it is the traditional costumes of the womenfolk that are far more flamboyant.*

LEFT AND BELOW
The burqa, *a stiff mask of black or gold coloured material, is the traditional face mask protecting women from the male gaze. Some choose to wear a veil although such covering is not compulsory in Islamic doctrine. (Below) colourfully clad local women dancing together while holding hands, running back and forth to the ululating chants*

Children of Dubai
are encouraged
to embrace their
heritage by retaining
traditional customs,
enabling them to
give context and
perspective to their
modern lifestyles.
The melding of the
old and new is a
particular charm
of Dubai. (left) a
small girl enters
her home through
the inner door.
Traditional homes in
Dubai were protected
with thick and heavy
-sometimes massive-
doors for defensive
purposes. Smaller,
inset doors were
the usual means of
entrance and exit into
and from the house.

RIGHT
The seal, or entrance
step of the door to
Hatta Fort guarded
by two friendly
keepers.

COMMERCE AND ENTERPRISE

PRECEDING PAGE
Ocean-going dhows *are still loaded at the wharf on the Creek as they have been for centuries, but today the process is facilitated by modern machinery.*

Dubai's seafaring legacy is still very much alive, and traditional dhows *such as these vessels are still used to transport passengers*

and cargo across the region. (right) An old pearling sambuk *is pictured here and (below) a crane hauls a dhow out of the water for repairs.*

The tiny pearl gave rise to an industry that dominated the lives of many generations of people in Dubai until the 1930s. Hassan Al Fardan (left and above) owns one of the largest collections of natural pearls in the world and is a leading authority on the Gulf pearl. His father, Haji Ibrahim Hassan Al Fardan, perfected the craft of drilling pearls and was known as the pearl doctor of the world.

LEFT
The Al Khattal boat factory near the Al Garhoud Bridge uses mostly traditional methods to build the expansive wooden rib cage of even the largest dhows. Hardwoods and mangrove poles are imported from India and East Africa to construct vessels of up to 44 metres long, capable of carrying 900 tons of cargo.

ABOVE
Craftsmen with traditional tools build the dhows with the experience of the eye, much as their ancestors have done for a thousand years or more.

LEFT AND ABOVE
Boats and boatmen busy till the setting sun, working their vessels.

RIGHT
Separating Deira from Bur Dubai, the Creek is a busy thoroughfare with dhows gliding up and down between a fleet of water taxis (abras) shuttling passengers back and forth from bank to bank.

Between the Al Maktoum Bridge and the Chamber of Commerce and Industry, expatriate workers load cargo onto waiting dhows. This shipment includes small diesel engines and pumps, brought by truck from Jeddah and bound for Somalia.

The camel has been the mainstay of life in trade and commerce across some of the harshest desert terrain in the world. Camel caravans passed through the region for thousands of years. So important is the animal to local cultures that the Arabs have given it the title Ata' Allah (Gift of Allah). Traditionally relying on desert sedges for nourishment, camels are now fed alfalfa grown specifically for them (lower right).

A far cry from the modern, air-conditioned shopping centres, the bustle of the covered passageways of Dubai's souks have always attracted a diverse collection of merchants and merchandise. Each commodity is quartered in specific areas, with shopkeepers competing eagerly for custom. (above) Porters still move goods in time-honoured fashion, as vegetable markets (right) display fresh, locally grown produce and (opposite page) old-style soothsayers and peddlers of future truths and worldly goods such as watches and rings, ply their trades in the old Deira perfume (atar) souk. A street of bright textiles suddenly becomes a row of tailors or small, cell-like shops stacked high with tinned or electrical goods.

ABOVE
This gold waistcoat, made-up of seven kilograms of gold and 53 carrots of diamonds, took 30 people six months to make and is on sale for a bargain 1.5 million Dirhams (US$4 million).

RIGHT
The glittering opulence of Dubai's Gold Souk along Sikkat Al Khail Street is famous throughout the world. Rows of shops are lined, floor to ceiling, with bracelets, necklaces, rings and ear-rings, more than half of which is imported from India, Saudi Arabia, Bahrain, Kuwait, Turkey, Singapore and Italy. Gold jewellery is sold by weight, with little charge made for the craftsmanship, and prices are fixed at the international daily gold rate.

FAITH

ABOVE
A Koran in the prayer hall of a mosque.

LEFT
The Ruling Family, Sheikhs and dignitaries perform the Eid prayer at the Bur Dubai Eid Musallah, with the ordinary citizenry. The bonds of Rulers and ruled are grounded in the positive tenets of Islam – modesty, respect and tolerance – which help to underwrite and strengthen many aspects of life in modern Dubai.

LEFT
Worshippers remove their shoes and wash before prayers, which are conducted kneeling down facing Mecca while bowing the head forward to touch the earth.

Dubai has a host of minarets pointing towards the heavens from some 200 mosques. Each neighbourhood has its own local mosque for weekday prayers, while many people gather at the larger mosques for the Friday prayers.

The first minarets in Islam were built in the eighth century 70 years after the Prophet's death, used as towers from which muezzins chanted the azzan - call to prayer - five times a day. (left) Hatta Mosque. (above) Jumeirah Mosque.

RESOURCE AND MOMENTUM

Dubai International Airport (DIA) and Emirates Airlines have been potent international symbols of Dubai's global success. Always looking to the future, the DIA and Emirates have consistently anticipated burgeoning demand with award-winning facilities and state-of-the-art services. Launched in 1985, Emirates Airlines has grown to become one of the world's most profitable and one of the 20 largest international carriers. Within two years of the Sheikh Rashid Terminal opening in 2000, the airport was handling over 15 million passengers a year, with 100 airlines operating over 10,000 scheduled flights a month. The current US$2.5 billion expansion of DIA incorporates a second runway, runway extensions, underground tunnels, new warehousing for Dubai Duty Free, a third passenger terminal and a Mega Cargo Terminal at Dubai Cargo Village.

The exploitation of oil and gas accelerated the rate of Dubai's transformation. The late Sheikh Rashid played the leading role in negotiations with the oil giants, and Dubai became the second largest oil producer in the UAE, with four major off-shore oilfields discovered between 1966 and 1976: Fateh, Southwest Fateh, Rashid and Falah, and an on-shore gas and condensate field at Margham.

Industry plays a
major role in the
development of
Dubai. Dubai
Aluminium (DUBAL)
is the largest such
facility in the Middle
East, producing
300,000 tons of
aluminium a year
and supplying 70
different products
to 250 customers
around the world.

PRECEDING PAGE
*The Jebel Ali
container port, the
largest in the Middle
East. As early as
1965 Sheikh Rashid
commissioned the
building of a four-
berth harbour –
Port Rashid – at the*
*mouth of the Creek
next to the city, using
a loan guaranteed by
future oil revenues.
By 1980, the port had
been enlarged to 35
berths and can today
handle up to 100
containers an hour.*

BELOW
Huge offshore platforms being built at Jebel Ali, the only such large-scale advanced heavy engineering works between Europe and the Far East.
The Dubai Dry Dock project, also launched by Sheikh Rashid, has become the biggest such facility between Europe and the Far East, currently repairing over 200 vessels a year from around the world.

152

Jebel Ali Docks and free trade zone helped increase Dubai's trade and service base, and broaden its economy to incorporate a vast and varied manufacturing base. Jebel Ali has the largest artificial harbour in the world and is one of the few man-made structures visible from space. Its 67 berths serve over 150 of the world's major container shipping lines and there are plans to further increase the number of berths to accommodate the steady growth in cargo traffic. The 15 kilometres of quays and two kilometres of wharfs include special zones for petroleum products, containers, dry bulk and forest products.

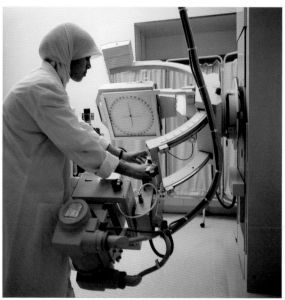

LEFT
Women are a growing percentage of the labour force in Dubai active in every field of endeavour. Here, a female technician at the Al Wasl Maternity Hospital in Dubai, readies equipment for a patient.

ABOVE AND RIGHT
A growing number of large modern hotels and shopping malls, like the Burjuman Shopping Centre (above) provide clean, spacious, air-conditioned environments with a range of goods and services matching the very best available in the world's major capital cities. The Twin Towers on Beniyas Road in Deira specialises in upmarket designer shops and afford panoramic views of the Creek from the balcony of the third floor food hall.

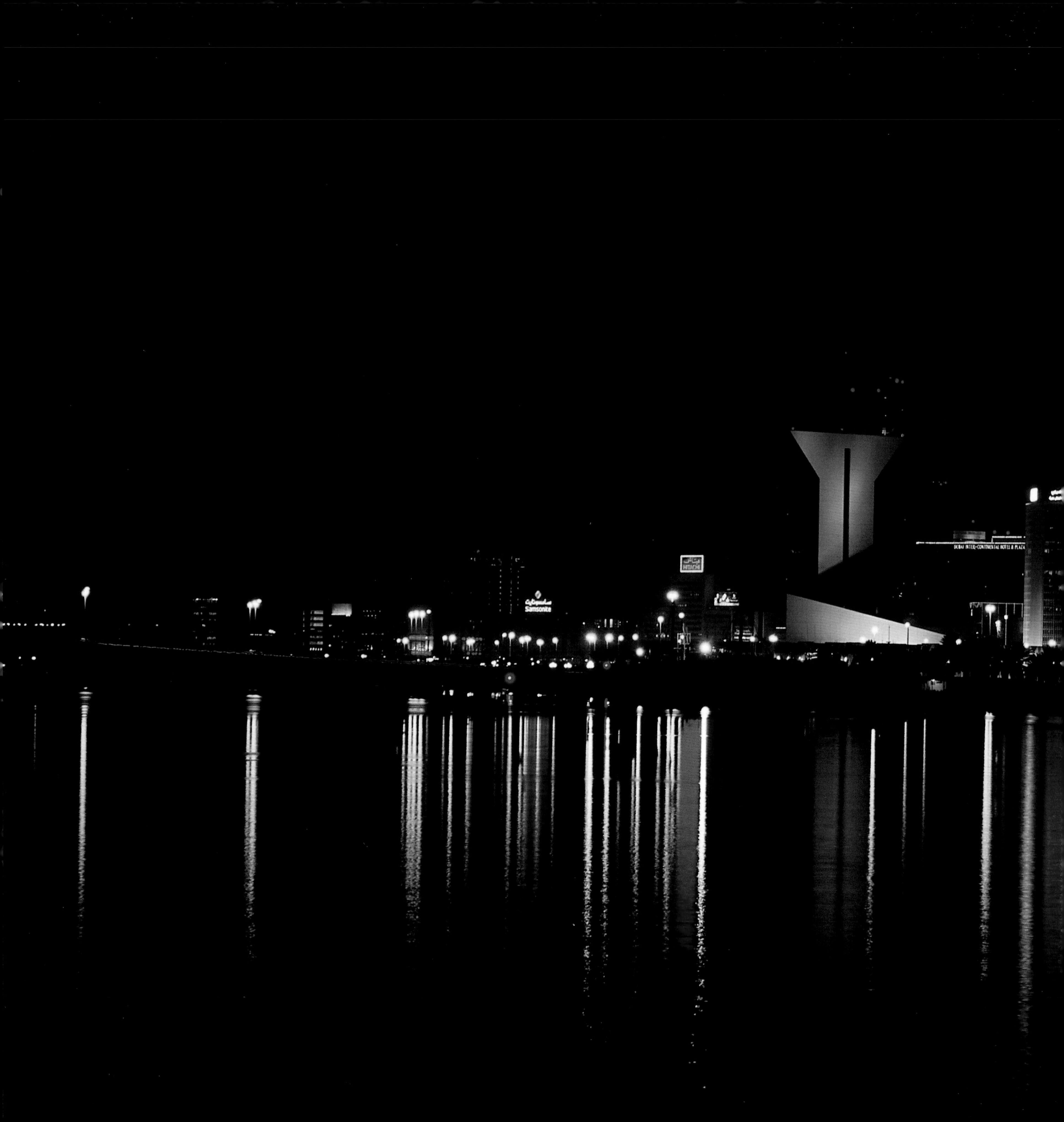
HITACHI
Samsonite
DUBAI INTER-CONTINENTAL HOTEL & PLAZA

MODERN DUBAI

In the past two decades Dubai has cultivated a confidence that is reflected in its architecture. As development moved up the Creek, building designs became ever more ambitious. (right) Since the late 1990s the stunning National Bank of Dubai building has towered over the chisel-shaped Chamber of Commerce and Industry, while the spidery Clock Tower (above) stands at one of the city's busiest intersections where the Al Maktoum Bridge traffic meets traffic travelling between the airport and Deira.

LEFT
City Tower 2 is one of a regiment of new high-rise towers that have relocated many of the city's major businesses from Deira to the Sheikh Zayed Road.

RIGHT
The two equilateral triangles of the Emirates Towers rise up from a central podium near the World Trade Centre. The taller tower houses prestige office suites, while its twin is a 400-room business hotel with conference centre, ballroom and executive facilities.

From the mid-1990s and continuing into the new millennium, a string of architecturally sophisticated towers have sprouted from the desert scrub lands along the Sheikh Zayed Road from the World Trade Centre (far right) towards the Abu Dhabi Highway. The Dusit building and hotel (left) and Hard Rock Café (above) were only a few years ago deemed to be outside the city limits. Today, development is racing towards Jebel Ali along the five-lane highway.

One of Dubai's landmark hotel developments of the 1990s, the Jumeirah Beach Hotel's extraordinary curving wave design is captured in all its sprawling splendour from this aerial view. In addition to the architectural novelty of curved corridors and an external sloping, wave-like structure, the Jumeirah Beach Hotel features a marina, conference centre, sports club and sandy private beaches.

Architects have incorporated traditional designs and motifs into many of the buildings in Dubai, enlivening interiors (left) with exotic settings in steel and glass reminiscent of desert oases built in the middle of hotels and shopping malls all over the city. The lobby of the Al Bustan Rotana Hotel reflects this decorative style.

RIGHT
The elegant, breaking-wave outline of the 26-storey Jumeirah Beach Hotel is complemented by the adjacent dhow-shaped conference centre with sail-like awnings, celebrating Dubai's maritime heritage.

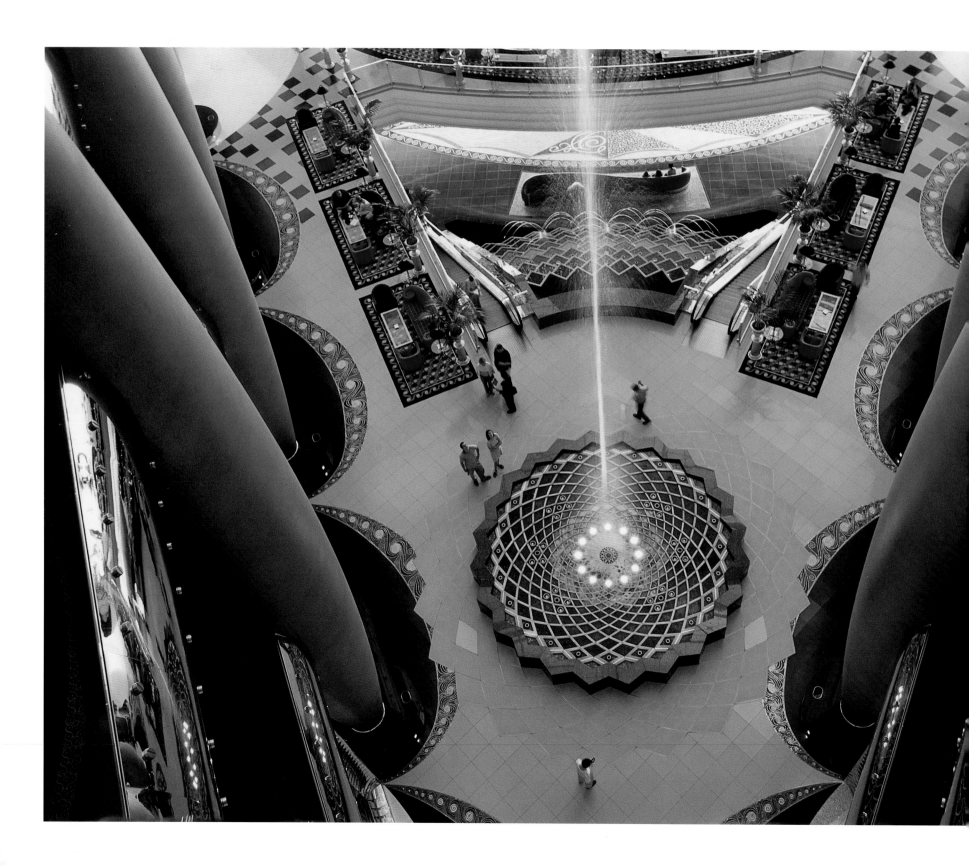

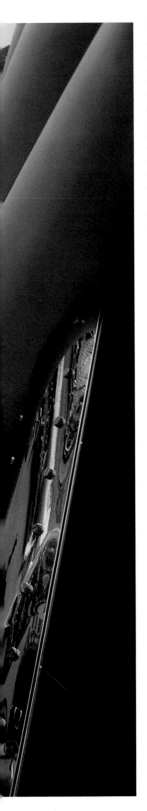

The sumptuous Burj Al Arab is the tallest hotel in the world. Its exterior (right) is constructed using double Teflon-coated glass fibre, while (left) the interior revels in its 2,000 square metres of 22-carat gold leaf adorned walls, pillars and domes. Each of the 202 all-duplex suites has floor-to-ceiling windows and a personal butler.

SPORT AND LEISURE

LEFT
The Creek Golf &
Yacht Club plays host
to the PGA Dubai
Desert Classic golf
tournament with
over US$1 million
in prize money.

BELOW
The Boardwalk
restaurant at the
Creek Golf & Yacht
Club is a favourite
watering hole for
locals and expatriate
business people,
and a perfect venue
from which to watch
the sun setting
over the Creek.

The Zabeel Riding Stables, owned by Crown Prince Sheikh Mohammed, began operating close to the World Trade Centre around 30 years ago. The present complex was set up in 1991 and is the first major racing stables in the UAE, with 120 racehorses currently in training. "Horses are a passion first, a business second," says internationally acclaimed trainer Satish Seemar who helped set up the stables. "Our horses receive top quality treatment, including nutrition and exercise, living like the princes that they are." Part of the daily exercise routine for these expensive equines involves regular training through therapeutic swims.

LEFT
Pride and beauty on display at the Zabeel Stables. "The horse is so indelibly linked with our culture, with all thoroughbreds in the world today tracing back to three Arabian horses which came from this part of the world, that it is only fitting that the best in the world return back to the region to challenge for the right to be called the best." Sheikh Maktoum bin Rashid Al Maktoum, Ruler of Dubai.

ABOVE
The Dubai World Cup was set up in 1996 and is the world's richest horse race with $15 million in prize money. Crown Prince Sheikh Mohammed, who is behind the project, is himself recognised as the world's largest breeder of fine thoroughbreds, with 3,000 horses in training around the world.

ABOVE
*The smell of success
as a champion
racehorse checks
out the trophies.*

Every Thursday from early October to mid-April races takes place at Nad Al Sheba (where the Dubai World Cup is held during the last week in March), attracting crowds of up to 35,000. Besides offering the best views of the racing, the Millennium Grandstand features a variety of hospitality options for day and night racing of champion horses and jockeys. The local people (right) are keen horse racing enthusiasts, making a day at the races with the family a familiar outing with picnics on the grass, watching (above) champion jockeys jockey for sport and reward, night and day.

LEFT
Polo has become a major sport of young entrepreneurs and successful businessmen in Dubai, with private and dedicated polo grounds and stables matching the very best in the world. Both men and women enjoy this exhilarating, but dangerous pastime. The Dubai Polo Club is a major venue for aficionados and holds matches throughout the winter.

ABOVE
Sheikh Mohammed, the Dubai Crown Prince, is a world-class endurance rider competing in championship events around the world all year round, despite his gruelling official duties. Winner of many trophies, he is here seen finishing a race hand in hand with one of his sons. Endurance races can cover 200 kilometres and more, over varied and arduous natural courses across desert terrain.

Originally a feature of large weddings and other celebrations, camel racing attracts a regular following in the Emirates, and substantial prize money, every Thursday and Friday throughout the winter. The specially designed racing tracks are several kilometres long to test the camels' legendary stamina. With the growth and popularity of camel racing, the Camel Reproduction Centre in Dubai has pioneered new breeding methods to produce animals of better genetic stock. There is even a major camel hospital in Dubai with surgery facilities and recuperative holding pens. Not surprising, given that some champion camels can fetch as much as their equine equivalents.

The desert spells unknown adventures for locals and tourists alike. The nearest large sand dunes to Dubai are at Qarn Nazwa on the road to Hatta, where dune driving (bashing) is a bone-jarring roller coaster ride on shifting sands and high dunes. Expert safari outfits like Arabian Adventures have experienced drivers who take tourists on unforgettable rides in Beau Geste country, camping out at nights under star-lit skies that seem almost to touch the face.

Sand skiing on a monoski is an exhilarating variation on snow boarding, but the lack of ski lifts necessitates an arduous climb back up to the top of the dune. Not a journey for the fainthearted.

RIGHT
Feliciano Lopez competing during the Dubai Men's Tennis Championship at the Dubai Tennis Stadium in February 2003.

LEFT
Contenders for the UIM Class 1 World Offshore Championship 2002 at the Mina Seyahi area, passing a section of Palm Island under construction.

RIGHT
Dhow sailing race in Dubai.

BELOW
Victory 7 during the UIM Class 1 World Offshore Championship 2002. Dubai has become a centre for the UIM World Championship races, the local Victory Team taking many trophies in races around the world.

VISION

Dubai is at the vanguard of modern Arab business centres eager to embrace modern technology. Dubai Internet City (DIC) provides a unique regional environment which encourages high-tech industries to operate out of the Emirates. Launched in October 2000, DIC has attracted many international companies, such as Microsoft, Oracle, Hewlett Packard, IBM and Compaq.

Combining tourism and conservation, the 29-suite, lodge-style Al Maha luxury resort is the first eco-tourism resort in the region. Within a protected environment in the heart of the desert, the Arabian oryx and other endangered species are being

re-introduced to their natural habitats. Al Maha is at the centre of a unique eco-system regeneration program that now encompasses 225 square kilometres as a fenced-off, protected conservation reserve, safeguarding nearly five per cent of Dubai's land and desert habitat.

LEFT

The Miami-style US$4.35 billion Dubai Marina, an Emaar property development, is being virtually scooped out of the Jumeirah coastline and desert. Intended to accommodate over 150,000 people in a mix of low, medium and high-rise buildings, the project is scheduled for completion in 2008. Like everything else in Dubai, the visitor is astonished at the appearance of such massive construction projects out of the desert, like mirages in the shimmering sand.

ABOVE

The transformation of desert lands and reclamation of the sea is intended to turn Dubai into the Monte Carlo of the Gulf region. The Palm Island projects at Jumeirah and Jebel Ali are the largest luxury housing developments in the world. Here, the setting sun reflects off the man-made crescent breakwater and the fast-forming tentacles of the Palm Island Jumeirah which will eventually accommodate 40 hotels, marinas, shopping plazas as well as luxury villas and high-rise apartment blocks.

Dubai's population more than doubled from 60,000 to 183,000 between 1970 and 1975 as the Emirate laid the foundations for rapid growth in a modern state. The swelling of the population to 1.1 million people is itself evidence of Dubai's dizzying rate of expansion. Today, Dubai is the most populace city in the Emirates, with an estimated one million people, almost double that of Abu Dhabi, the UAE's capital city.

ABOVE
The falcon is the national symbol of the United Arab Emirates.

RIGHT
A man of vision, General Sheikh Mohammed bin Rashid Al Maktoum, Dubai Crown Prince and UAE Minister of Defence.

CREDITS

INDEX

206

PHOTOGRAPHY CREDITS AND BIBLIOGRAPHY

David Saunders:

2, 4-5, 8, 9, 10-11, 12, 13, 14-15, 16, 18-19, 34, 38-39, 54-55, 58, 60 (left), 62, 76, 80, 83, 84, 89, 90, 91, 92, 93 (top), 96-97, 99 (right), 100 (right), 103 (right), 105 (right), 106, 109 (top & right), 114-115, 116, 117, 118, 119, 120, 121 (both), 122 (right), 123, 124 (both), 125, 126, 127 (right & btm), 128 (btm), 132, 133, 136 (top), 137, 138, 139, 140-141, 142, 143, 144 (right), 145, 150, 151, 152, 153, 155, 156-157, 158, 159, 160, 161, 162 (left), 163, 165, 168 (top), 169, 170, 171, 176, 177, 178, 179, 180 (top), 181, 196.

Darius Zandi:

17, 68-69, 72, 73, 77, 78, 86-87, 88 (both), 93 (btm) 94, 95, 98, 99 (left), 100 (left), 101, 102, 103 (left), 104, 107 (all), 108, 109 (btm left), 110, 111 (both), 112, 113, 122 (left), 127 (left), 128 (top), 129, 130-131, 134-135, 144 (left), 148-149, 154 (both), 162, 164 (left), 166-167, 168 (btm left), 175, 188, 189 (btm), 190, 194-195, 202-203.

Gulf News:

20, 48 (left & top right), 50 (both), 52, 61, 63, 64, 65 (btm right), 66-67, 136 (btm), 146, 147, 172-173, 174, 182, 183, 184, 191, 192 (both), 193, 198, 199.

Ronald Codrai:

21, 22, 23, 25, 27, 28, 32, 33, 35, 36, 41, 45, 200.

Marijke Jongbloed:

70, 71 (both), 74, 75 (all), 79, 81, 82, 85.

Rik Van Lent:

48 (btm), 105 (top), 180 (btm), 185, 186-187, 189 (right), 201.

Dubai Department of Civil Aviation:

46 (both), 53 (both), 59, 60 (right).

National Bank of Dubai:

24-25, 57.

Emirates:

197.

DIFC:

65 (top right).

Arabian Sands
by Wilfred Thesiger (1959)
Harper Collins, 2000.

Dubai
Lonely Planet Publications, 2000.

Dubai: An Arabian Album
by Ronald Codrai
UAE, 1992.

Dubai: A Pictorial Tour
Motivate Publishing, 1996.

Fabled Cities, Princes and Jinn, from Arab Myths and Legends
text by Khairat Al-Saleh
Eurobook Ltd, 1985.

Father of Dubai: Sheikh Rashid bin Saeed Al Maktoum
by Graeme Wilson
Media Prima, 1999.

From Trucial States to United Arab Emirates
by Frauke Heard-Bey
Longman, 1982, third impression 1999.

Images of Dubai and the United Arab Emirates
Explorer Publishing, 2002.

Insight Pocket Guide: Dubai
by Matt Jones
APA Publications, 2002.

Oman & the United Arab Emirates
Lonely Planet Publications, 2000.

Phoenix Rising: 25 years of the United Arab Emirates
edited by Michael Asher
HA International Associates Ltd, 1996.

Phoenix Rising: The United Arab Emirates, Past, Present & Future
by Michael Asher, photography by Werner Forman
Harvill Press, 1996.

Rashid: the Man Behind Dubai
by Abbas Abdullah Makki
Reading For All, 1990.

The Koran
translated with notes by N.J. Dawood
Penguin, 1956, revised 1990.

The Pelican History of the World
by J.M. Roberts
Penguin Books Ltd., 1981.

The Seven Voyages of Sinbad the Sailor
retold by John Yeoman
Pavilion Books, 1996.

The Wells of Memory: An Autobiography
by Easa Saleh Al-Gurg, CBE
John Murray, 1998.

United Arab Emirates Yearbook
Trident Press, 2003.

ACKNOWLEDGEMENTS

The Publishers wish to give special thanks to Mr. Abdullah M. Saleh, Managing Director, and the National Bank of Dubai for their support. Further thanks are due to Mr. Doug Dowie, Mr. Saleem Shariffee and Walid Al Masri at the NBD.

Our thanks extend to Mr. Mohammed Al Gergawi, Chairman of the Executive Office and to Mr. Habib Al Redha, the Under Secretary, Ministry of Information, Dubai for their guidance.

Our gratitude is due to the Dubai Department of Civil Aviation and Ms. Anita Mehra, and to Kifah Saleh and Masoud M. Saleh.

Darius Zandi and Marijke Jongbloed deserve our thanks for their co-operation and splendid photography. Francis Matthew at Gulf News, with Mhic Chambers and Abdul Kareem, have ably assisted in the completion of our photography.

Roger Fawcett-Tang and Struktur Design deserve much credit for making this volume unsurpassed in stylistic content and design work. Caroline Clarke's initial design concepts also deserve our thanks.

Many people inside and outside of Dubai have helped make this book possible, but we owe the principal debt of gratitude to Mr. Hossein Amirsadeghi for his inspiration and creation of this volume.

The authors also wish to thank Lucy Blogg (Department of Tourism and Commerce Marketing), Roddy Gordon (Grand Hyatt), Solena Le Sann & Marta Bencikova (Royal Mirage), Anne Bleeker and Mia (Jumeirah International), Claudio Campolucci and Colin Vincent (Hatta Fort Hotel), Tony Williams (Al Maha), Frédéric Bardin (Arabian Adventures), David Snelling (Emirates Airlines), Satish Seemar (Zabeel Racing Stables), Sean Cronin (VIP Helicopters), Hassan Al Fardan, Mustafa Al Fardan, Mohammed and Redha Al Fardan, David Stead, Shakir, Thomas & Blessy Matthews and David Miller.